SHURLEY ENGLISH

HOMESCHOOL MADE EASY

LEVEL 5

Student Book

By

Brenda Shurley

Shurley Instructional Materials, Inc., Cabot, Arkansas

03-13
Shurley English Homeschooling
Level 5 Student Workbook
ISBN 978-1-58561-033-4

Printed in the United States of America by RR Donnelley, Owensville, MO.

For additional information or to place an order, write to: Shurley Instructional Materials, Inc.
366 SIM Drive
Cabot, AR 72023

1 2 3 4 5 6 7 8   13 11 09 08 06 05 03 01

JINGLE

SECTION

Jingle Section

Jingle 1: Noun Jingle

Yo! Ho! It's the NOUN we know!
A noun names a person;
A noun names a place;
A noun names a person, place, or thing,
And sometimes an idea!
Person, Place, Thing, Idea.

Finding nouns is a game.
Listen now to the nouns we name:
Head, shoulders, knees, and toes,
Girls, boys, shoes, and clothes.

Yo! Ho! It's the NOUN we know!
Yo! Ho! It's the NOUN we know!
Person, Place, Thing, Idea.
Person, Place, Thing, Idea.
Now, it's time to say Yo! Whoa!

Jingle 2: Verb Jingle

A verb, a verb. What is a verb?
Haven't you heard?
There are two kinds of verbs:
The action verb and the linking verb.

The action verb shows a state of action,
Like **stand** and **sit** and **smile**.
The action verb is always doing
Because it tells what the subject does.
We **stand**! We **sit**! We **smile**!

The linking verb is a state of being,
Like **am, is, are, was**, and **were**,
Look, become, grows, and **feels**.
A linking verb shows no action
Because it tells what the subject is.
He **is** *a clown.* *He* **looks** *funny.*

Jingle 3: Sentence Jingle

A sentence, sentence, sentence
Is complete, complete, complete
When 5 simple rules
It meets, meets, meets.

It has a subject, subject, subject
And a verb, verb, verb.
It makes sense, sense, sense
With every word, word, word.

Add a capital letter, letter
And an end mark, mark.
Now, we're finished, and aren't we smart!
Now, our sentence has all its parts!

REMEMBER
Subject, Verb, Com-plete sense,
Capital letter, and an end mark, too.
That's what a sentence is all about!

Jingle 4: Adverb Jingle

An adverb modifies a verb, adjective, or another adverb.
An adverb asks *How? When? Where?*
To find an adverb: **Go, Ask, Get.**
Where do I **go**? To a verb, adjective, or another adverb.
What do I **ask**? How? When? Where?
What do I **get**? An ADVERB! (Clap) That's what!

Jingle 5: Adjective Jingle

An adjective modifies a noun or pronoun.
An adjective asks *What kind? Which one? How many*?
To find an adjective: **Go, Ask, Get**.
Where do I **go**? To a noun or pronoun.
What do I **ask**? What kind? Which one? How many?
What do I **get**? An ADJECTIVE! (Clap) That's what!

Jingle Section

Jingle 6: Article Adjective Jingle

We are the article adjectives,
Teeny, tiny adjectives:
A, AN, THE - A, AN, THE.

We are called article adjectives and noun markers;
We are memorized and used every day.
So, if you spot us, you can mark us
With the label A.

We are the article adjectives,
Teeny, tiny adjectives:
A, AN, THE - A, AN, THE.

Jingle 7: The Preposition Jingle

A PREP PREP PREPOSITION
Is a special group of words
That connects a
NOUN, NOUN, NOUN
Or a PRO, PRO, PRONOUN
To the rest of the sentence.

Jingle 8: Object of the Prep Jingle

Dum De Dum Dum!
An O-P is a N-O-U-N or a P-R-O
After the P-R-E-P
In a S-E-N-T-E-N-C-E.
Dum De Dum Dum - DONE!!

Jingle 9: Preposition Flow Jingle

1. **Preposition, Preposition**
Starting with an A.
(Fast)
aboard, about, above,
across, after, against,
(Slow)
along, among, around, at.

2. **Preposition, Preposition**
Starting with a B.
(Fast)
before, behind, below,
beneath, beside, between,
(Slow)
beyond, but, by.

3. **Preposition, Preposition**
Starting with a D.
down (slow & long),
during (snappy).

4. **Preposition, Preposition**
Don't go away.
Go to the middle
And see what we say.
E-F-I and L-N-O
except, for, from,
in, inside, into,
like,
near, of, off,
on, out, outside, over.

5. **Preposition, Preposition**
Almost through.
Start with P and end with W.
past, since, through,
throughout, to, toward,
under, underneath,
until, up, upon,
with, within, without.

6. **Preposition, Preposition**
Easy as can be.
We're all finished,
And aren't you pleased?
We've just recited
All 49 of these.

Jingle 10: Pronoun Jingle

These little pronouns,
Hanging around,
Take the place of all the nouns.
With a smile and a nod
And a twinkle of the eye,
Give those pronouns
a big high-five! Yea!

Jingle 11: Subject Pronoun Jingle

There are seven subject pronouns
That are easy as can be:
I and we,   (clap twice)
He and she,   (clap twice)
It and they and you.   (clap three)

Jingle Section

Jingle 12: Possessive Pronoun Jingle

There are seven possessive pronouns
That are easy as can be:
My and our,   (clap twice)
His and her,   (clap twice)
Its and their and your.   (clap twice)

Jingle 13: Object Pronoun Jingle

There are seven object pronouns
That are easy as can be:
Me and us,   (clap twice)
Him and her,   (clap twice)
It and them and you.   (clap three)

Jingle 14: The 23 Helping Verbs of the Mean, Lean Verb Machine Jingle

These 23 helping verbs will be on my test.
I gotta remember them so I can do my best.
I'll start out with 8 and finish with 15;
Just call me the mean, lean verb machine.

There are 8 **be** verbs that are easy as can be:
   am, is, are – was and were,
   am, is, are – was and were,
   am, is, are – was and were,
   be, being, and been.
All together now, the 8 **be** verbs:
am, is, are – was and were – be, being, and been,
am, is, are – was and were – be, being, and been.

There're 23 helping verbs, and I've recited only 8.
That leaves fifteen more that I must relate:
   has, have, and had – do, does, and did,
   has, have, and had – do, does, and did,
   might, must, may – might, must, may.

Knowing these verbs will save my grade:
   can and could – would and should,
   can and could – would and should,
   shall and will,
   shall and will.
In record time, I did this drill.
I'm the mean, lean verb machine – STILL!

Jingle 15: Eight Parts of Speech Jingle

Want to know how to write?
Use the eight parts of speech - They're dynamite!

Nouns, **V**erbs, and **P**ronouns - They rule!
They're called the **NVP's**, and they're really cool!
The **Double A's** are on the move;
Adjectives and **A**dverbs help you groove!
Next come the **PIC's**, and then we're done!
The **PIC's** are **P**reposition, **I**nterjection, and **C**onjunction!

All together now, the eight parts of speech, abbreviations please:
NVP, AA, PIC   NVP, AA, PIC!

Jingle 16: Direct Object Jingle

1. A direct object is a noun or pronoun.

2. A direct object completes the meaning of the sentence.

3. A direct object is located after the verb-transitive.

4. To find the direct object, ask WHAT or WHOM after your verb.

Jingle Section

Jingle 17: Indirect Object Jingle
1. An indirect object is a noun or pronoun.
2. An indirect object receives what the direct object names.
3. An indirect object is located between the verb-transitive and the direct object.
4. To find the indirect object, ask TO WHOM or FOR WHOM after the direct object.

Jingle 18: Predicate Noun Jingle
1. A predicate noun is a noun or a pronoun.
2. A predicate noun means the same thing as the subject word.
3. A predicate noun is located after a linking verb.
4. To find the predicate noun, ask WHAT or WHO after the verb.

Jingle 19: Another Predicate Noun Jingle	
Listen, my comrades, and you shall hear About predicate nouns from far and near. No one knows the time or year When the predicate nouns will appear. Listen now to all the facts, So you will know when the **Pred's** are back!	Dum De Dum Dum! **A pred**icate noun is a special noun in the predicate That means the same thing as the subject word. **To find a pred**icate noun, ask *what* or *who* After a linking verb.

Notes

REFERENCE

SECTION

Vocabulary Reference

Chapter 1, Vocabulary Words #1	Chapter 1, Vocabulary Words #2
(construction, dilapidation, prodigy, genius)	(audacious, timid, abolish, destroy)

Chapter 2, Vocabulary Words #1	Chapter 2, Vocabulary Words #2
(authentic, false, acknowledge, admit)	(withhold, bequeath, pardon, amnesty)

Chapter 3, Vocabulary Words #1	Chapter 3, Vocabulary Words #2
(conceal, exhume, mimic, imitate)	(fact, hypothesis, debate, argue)

Chapter 4, Vocabulary Words #1	Chapter 4, Vocabulary Words #2
(coherent, ramble, deception, fraud)	(colleague, competitor, vacant, void)

Chapter 5, Vocabulary Words #1	Chapter 5, Vocabulary Words #2
(alliance, division, frugal, thrifty)	(melodramatic, subdued, odious, hateful)

Chapter 6, Vocabulary Words #1	Chapter 6, Vocabulary Words #2
(veritable, fictitious, perpetual, constant)	(ethical, carnal, prodigal, wasteful)

Chapter 7, Vocabulary Words #1	Chapter 7, Vocabulary Words #2
(frivolous, grave, proverbial, notorious)	(vague, specific, transparent, translucent)

Chapter 8, Vocabulary Words #1	Chapter 8, Vocabulary Words #2
(myth, fact, veracity, truth)	(spurious, accurate, condense, abbreviate)

Chapter 9, Vocabulary Words #1	Chapter 9, Vocabulary Words #2
(simultaneous, periodic, odd, quaint)	(savory, bland, honesty, integrity)

Chapter 10, Vocabulary Words #1	Chapter 10, Vocabulary Words #2
(spontaneous, forced, burn, smolder)	(repulsive, amiable, escalate, expand)

Chapter 11, Vocabulary Words #1	Chapter 11, Vocabulary Words #2
(solicitude, indifference, mandatory, required)	(reprehensible, admirable, knoll, mound)

Chapter 12, Vocabulary Words #1	Chapter 12, Vocabulary Words #2
(marginal, significant, ecstatic, blissful)	(precarious, stable, zeppelin, balloon)

Chapter 13, Vocabulary Words #1	Chapter 13, Vocabulary Words #2
(luminous, obscure, bangle, bracelet)	(innate, acquired, entourage, followers)

Chapter 14, Vocabulary Words #1	Chapter 14, Vocabulary Words #2
(impenetrable, vulnerable, equestrian, rider)	(cordial, hostile, equilibrium, balance)

Chapter 15, Vocabulary Words #1	Chapter 15, Vocabulary Words #2
(gullible, dubious, fatigue, exhaustion)	(gaudy, tasteful, grandiose, impressive)

Vocabulary Reference

Chapter 16, Vocabulary Words #1	Chapter 16, Vocabulary Words #2
(flippant, polite, camouflage, conceal)	(exquisite, gauche, scrutinize, examine)

Chapter 17, Vocabulary Words #1	Chapter 17, Vocabulary Words #2
(diligent, negligent, contemplate, ponder)	(delusion, reality, enunciation, pronounce)

Chapter 18, Vocabulary Words #1	Chapter 18, Vocabulary Words #2
(deception, candor, forfeit, relinquish)	(vanquish, escape, solitary, alone)

Chapter 19, Vocabulary Words #1	Chapter 19, Vocabulary Words #2
(contemptible, admirable, adversity, misfortune)	(conceited, humble, creditor, lender)

Chapter 20, Vocabulary Words #1	Chapter 20, Vocabulary Words #2
(component, whole, expense, disbursement)	(candid, sly, mandatory, required)

Chapter 21, Vocabulary Words #1	Chapter 21, Vocabulary Words #2
(brusque, diplomatic, amateur, beginner)	(superficial, genuine, aggressive, hostile)

Chapter 22, Vocabulary Words #1	Chapter 22, Vocabulary Words #2
(summit, base, attire, apparel)	(repeal, pass, chaperon, escort)

Chapter 23, Vocabulary Words #1	Chapter 23, Vocabulary Words #2
(reconcile, sever, reimburse, refund)	(provoke, pacify, reputable, honest)

Chapter 24, Vocabulary Words #1	Chapter 24, Vocabulary Words #2
(noble, paltry, repulsive, vile)	(notorious, reputed, solitary, alone)

Reference 1: Beginning Setup Plan for Homeschool

You should use this plan to keep things in order!

1. Have separate color-coded pocket folders for each subject.
2. Put unfinished work in the right-hand side and finished work in the left-hand side of each subject folder.
3. Put notes to study, graded tests, and study guides in the brads so you will have them to study for scheduled tests.
4. Have a paper folder to store extra clean sheets of paper. Keep it full at all times.
5. Have an assignment folder to be reviewed every day.

Things to keep in your assignment folder:

A. Keep a monthly calendar of assignments, test dates, report-due dates, project-due dates, extra activities, dates and times, review dates, etc.

B. Keep a grade sheet to record the grades received in each subject. (*You might also consider keeping your grades on the inside cover of each subject folder. However you keep your grades, just remember to keep up with them accurately. Your grades are your business, so keep up with them! Grades help you know which areas need attention.*)

C. Make a list every day of the things you want to do so you can keep track of what you finish and what you do not finish. Move the unfinished items to your new list the next day. (*Yes, making this list takes time, but it's your road map to success. You will always know at a glance what you set out to accomplish and what still needs to be done.*)

6. Keep all necessary school supplies in a handy, heavy-duty Ziploc bag or a pencil bag.

Reference 2: Synonyms, Antonyms, and Six-Step Vocabulary Plan

Part 1: Synonyms and Antonyms

Definitions: Synonyms are words that have similar or almost the same meanings.
Antonyms are words that have opposite meanings.

Directions: Identify each pair of words as synonyms or antonyms by putting parentheses ( ) around **syn** or **ant**.

1. brisk, swift   **(syn)**   ant   2. dusk, nightfall   **(syn)**   ant   3. gentle, callous   syn   **(ant)**

Part 2: Six-Step Vocabulary Plan

(1) Write a title for the vocabulary words in each chapter.
Example: **Chapter 1, Vocabulary Words**

(2) Write each vocabulary word in your vocabulary notebook.

(3) Look up each vocabulary word in a dictionary or thesaurus.

(4) Write the meaning beside each vocabulary word.

(5) Write a sentence that helps you remember how each vocabulary word is used.

(6) Write and identify a pair of synonym words and a pair of antonym words.

Reference 3: What is Journal Writing?

Journal Writing is a written record of your personal thoughts and feelings about things or people that are important to you. Recording your thoughts in a journal is a good way to remember how you felt about what was happening in your life at a particular time. You can record your dreams, memories, feelings, and experiences. You can ask questions and answer some of them. It is fun to go back later and read what you have written because it shows how you have changed in different areas of your life. A journal can also be an excellent place to look for future writing topics, creative stories, poems, etc. Writing in a journal is an easy and enjoyable way to practice your writing skills without worrying about a writing grade.

What do I write about?

Journals are personal, but sometimes it helps to have ideas to get you started. Remember, in a journal, you do not have to stick to one topic. Write about someone or something you like. Write about what you did last weekend or on vacation. Write about what you hope to do this week or on your next vacation. Write about home, school, friends, hobbies, special talents (yours or someone else's), present and future hopes and fears. Write about what is wrong in your world and what you would do to "fix" it. Write about the good things and the bad things in your world. If you think about a past event and want to write an opinion about it now, put it in your journal. If you want to give your opinion about a present or future event that could have an impact on your life or the way that you see things, put it in your journal. If something bothers you, record it in your journal. If something interests you, record it. If you just want to record something that doesn't seem important at all, write it in your journal. After all, it is your journal!

How do I get started writing in my personal journal?

You need to put the day's date on the title line of your paper: **Month, Day, Year.** Skip the next line and begin your entry. You might write one or two sentences, a paragraph, a whole page, or several pages. Except for the journal date, no particular organizational style is required for journal writing. You decide how best to organize and express your thoughts. Feel free to include sketches, diagrams, lists, etc., if they will help you remember your thoughts about a topic or an event. You will also need a spiral notebook, a pen, a quiet place, and at least 5-10 minutes of uninterrupted writing time.

Note: Use a pen if possible. Pencils have lead points that break and erasers, both of which slow down your thoughts. Any drawings you might include do not have to be masterpieces—stick figures will do nicely.

Reference 4: This reference is located on page 11.

Reference 5: This reference is located on page 12.

Reference 6: The Four Kinds of Sentences and the End Mark Flow

1. A **declarative** sentence makes a statement.
   It is labeled with a **D**.
   Example: Sarah played tennis today.
   (Period, statement, declarative sentence)

2. An **imperative** sentence gives a command.
   It is labeled with an **Imp**.
   Example: Put your shoes in your closet.
   (Period, command, imperative sentence)

3. An **interrogative** sentence asks a question.
   It is labeled with an **Int**.
   Example: Did you see the new teacher?
   (Question mark, question, interrogative sentence)

4. An **exclamatory** sentence expresses strong feeling.
   It is labeled with an **E**.
   Example: The spider is on Jamie!
   (Exclamation point, strong feeling, exclamatory sentence)

Examples: Read each sentence, recite the End Mark Flow in parentheses, and put the end mark and the abbreviation for the sentence type in the blank at the end of each sentence.

1. Jerry cooked his supper **. D**
   (*Period, statement, declarative sentence*)

2. The snake slithered toward me **! E**
   (*Exclamation point, strong feeling, exclamatory sentence*)

3. Put your homework on the desk **. Imp**
   (*Period, command, imperative sentence*)

4. Are they going to the movies **? Int**
   (*Question mark, question, interrogative sentence*)

Reference 4: Checklists

Revision Checklist

1. Eliminate unnecessary or needlessly repeated words or ideas.
2. Combine or reorder sentences.
3. Change word choices for clarity and expression.
4. Know the purpose: to explain, to describe, to entertain, or to persuade.
5. Know the audience: the reader(s) of the writing.

Beginning Editing Checklist

1. Did you indent the paragraph?
2. Did you capitalize the first word and put an end mark at the end of every sentence?
3. Did you spell words correctly?

More Editing Skills

4. Did you follow the writing guidelines? (*located in Reference 13 on student page 13*)
5. Did you list the topic and three points on separate lines at the top of the paper?
6. Did you follow the three-point paragraph pattern?
7. Did you write in the point of view assigned? (*first or third person*)
8. Did you use the correct homonyms?
9. Did you follow all other capitalization and punctuation rules?
10. Did you follow the three-paragraph essay pattern?

Final Paper Checklist

1. Have you written the correct heading on your paper?
2. Have you written your final paper in ink?
3. Have you single-spaced your final paper?
4. Have you written your final paper neatly?
5. Have you stapled the final paper to the rough draft and handed them in to your teacher?

Writing Process Checklist

1. Gather information.
2. Write a rough draft.
3. Revise the rough draft.
4. Edit the rough draft.
5. Write a final paper.

Reference 7: Additional Article Adjective Information

1. **A/An** are called <u>indefinite</u> articles, meaning one of several.
   (Examples: **a** candy cane—**an** apron.)

2. **The** is called a <u>definite</u> article, meaning the only one there is.
   (Examples: **the** candy cane—**the** apron.)

3. The article **The** has two pronunciations:

   a. As a long **e** (*where the article precedes a word that begins with a vowel sound: the elephant, the iguana*)

   b. As a short **u** (*where the article precedes a word that begins with a consonant sound: the party, the dress*)

Reference 5: Paragraph Samples

Rough Draft

When Melissa arrived, at the airport last weak, the people was so thick that she could hardly move. Melissa quickly moved through the airports crowded hallways, because she was already late. She arrived at the right terminial just in time to bored her flight. Melissa was out of breath and her hart was beating hard too. When she reached her seat on the plain, she was tired. Before she fell asleep she promised to allow extra time for the large crowds.

Revision of Draft

When Melissa arrived, at the airport last weak, the people was so thick she could **barely** move. **Because she was already late, Melissa rushed through the airports crowded corridors.** She arrived at the **correct** terminial just in time to bored her flight. Melissa was out of breath and **her hart was pounding rapidly from her mad dash through the airport**. When she finally reached her seat on the plain, she was **exhausted**. Before she fell asleep she promised to allow extra time for the **enormous** crowds **at the airport**.

Edit Draft

When Melissa arrived [**delete comma**] at the airport last week, [**week, not weak**] the people were [**were, not was**] so thick she could barely move. Because she was already late, Melissa rushed through the airport's [**apostrophe added**] crowded corridors. She arrived at the correct terminal [**terminal, not terminial**] just in time to board [**board, not bored**] her flight. Melissa was out of breath, [**comma inserted**] and her heart [**heart, not hart**] was pounding rapidly from her mad dash through the airport. When she finally reached her seat on the plane, [**plane, not plain**] she was exhausted. Before she fell asleep, [**comma inserted**] she promised to allow extra time for the enormous crowds at the airport.

Final Paragraph

When Melissa arrived at the airport last week, the people were so thick she could barely move. Because she was already late, Melissa rushed through the airport's crowded corridors. She arrived at the correct terminal just in time to board her flight. Melissa was out of breath, and her heart was pounding rapidly from her mad dash through the airport. When she finally reached her seat on the plane, she was exhausted. Before she fell asleep, she promised to allow extra time for the enormous crowds at the airport.

Reference 8: Question and Answer Flow Sentence

Question and Answer Flow Sentence: The determined competitors swam feverishly.

1. Who swam feverishly? competitors - SN
2. What is being said about competitors? competitors swam - V
3. Swam how? feverishly - Adv
4. What kind of competitors? determined - Adj
5. The - A

Classified Sentence: A   Adj   SN   V   Adv
The determined competitors swam feverishly.

Reference 9: Question and Answer Flow Sentence

Question and Answer Flow for Sentence: The exquisite diamond sparkled brightly.

1. What sparkled brightly? diamond - SN
2. What is being said about diamond? diamond sparkled - V
3. Sparkled how? brightly - Adv
4. What kind of diamond? exquisite - Adj
5. The - A
6. SN V P1 Check
   (Say: Subject Noun, Verb, Pattern 1, Check)
7. Period, statement, declarative sentence
8. Go back to the verb - divide the complete subject from the complete predicate.

Classified Sentence: A   Adj   SN   V   Adv
SN V   The exquisite diamond / sparkled brightly. **D**
P1

Reference 10: Definitions for a Skill Builder Check

1. A **noun** names a person, place, thing, or idea.

2. A **singular noun** usually does not end in an *s* or *es* and means only one. (*truck, pencil, plane*)
   Exception: Some nouns that end in s are singular and mean only one. (*glass-glasses, dress-dresses*)

3. A **plural noun** usually ends in an *s* or *es* and means more than one. (*trucks, pencils, planes*)
   Exception: Some nouns are made plural by changing their spelling. (*man-men, child-children*)

4. A **common noun** names ANY person, place, or thing. A common noun is not capitalized because it does not name a specific person, place, or thing. (*tiger, yard*)

5. A **proper noun** is a noun that names a specific, or particular, person, place, or thing. Proper nouns are always capitalized no matter where they are located in the sentence. (*Keith, Alaska*)

6. A **simple subject** is another name for the subject noun or subject pronoun.

7. A **simple predicate** is another name for the verb.

Reference 11: Noun Job Chart

Directions: Look at the classified sentence below and underline the complete subject once and the complete predicate twice. Then, complete the table.

```
            A    Adj     SN        V     Adv    Adv
1. SN V     The angry teenager / stormed loudly upstairs. D
   P1
```

List the Noun Used	List the Noun Job	Singular or Plural	Common or Proper	Simple Subject	Simple Predicate
teenager	SN	S	C	teenager	stormed

Reference 12: Adverb Exception

(The famous actor **suddenly / collapsed**.) To show the adverb exception: (The famous actor **/ suddenly collapsed**.)

To add the adverb exception to the Question and Answer Flow, say, "*Is there an adverb exception?*" If there is not an adverb before the verb you say, "*No.*" If there is an adverb before the verb, you say, "*Yes - change the line.*"

Reference 13: Writing Guidelines

1. Label your writing assignment in the top right-hand corner of your page with the following information:
   A. Your Name
   B. The Writing Assignment Number (*Example: WA#1, WA#2, etc.*)
   C. Type of Writing (*Examples: Expository Paragraph, Persuasive Essay, Descriptive Paragraph, etc.*)
   D. The title of the writing on the top of the first line

2. Think about the topic that you are assigned.

3. Think about the type of writing assigned, which is the purpose for the writing.
   (*Is your writing intended to explain, persuade, describe, or narrate?*)

4. Think about the writing format, which is the organizational plan you are expected to use.
   (*Is your assignment a paragraph, a 3-paragraph essay, a 5-paragraph essay, or a letter?*)

5. Use your writing time wisely.
   (*Begin work quickly and concentrate on your assignment until it is finished.*)

Reference 14: Three-Point Paragraph Example

Topic: **My favorite foods**

Three main points: 1. **pizza** 2. **hamburgers** 3. **ice cream**

Sentence #1 – <u>Topic Sentence</u> (*Use words in the topic and tell how many points will be used.*)
I have three favorite foods.

Sentence #2 – <u>3-Point Sentence</u> (*List the 3 points in the order you will present them.*)
These foods are pizza, hamburgers, and ice cream.

Sentence #3 – <u>First Point</u>
My first favorite food is pizza.

Sentence #4 – <u>Supporting Sentence</u> for the first point.
I like pizza because of its great Italian taste.

Sentence #5 – <u>Second Point</u>
My second favorite food is hamburgers.

Sentence #6 – <u>Supporting Sentence</u> for the second point.
To me, the best kind is the hamburger that has all the trimmings, even onions.

Sentence #7 – <u>Third Point</u>
My third favorite food is ice cream.

Sentence #8 – <u>Supporting Sentence</u> for the third point.
I love ice cream because I love sweet, creamy things to eat.

Sentence #9 – <u>Concluding (final) Sentence</u> (*Restate the topic sentence and add an extra thought.*)
I enjoy eating all kinds of foods, but my favorites will probably always be pizza, hamburgers, and ice cream.

SAMPLE PARAGRAPH:

My Favorite Foods

I have three favorite foods. These foods are pizza, hamburgers, and ice cream. My first favorite food is pizza. I like pizza because of its great Italian taste. My second favorite food is hamburgers. To me, the best kind is the hamburger that has all the trimmings, even onions. My third favorite food is ice cream. I love ice cream because I love sweet, creamy things to eat. I enjoy eating all kinds of foods, but my favorites will probably always be pizza, hamburgers, and ice cream.

Reference 15: Natural and Inverted Word Order

A **Natural Order** sentence has all subject parts first and all predicate parts after the verb. **Inverted Order** means that a sentence has predicate words in the complete subject. When a word is located in the complete subject but modifies the verb, it is a predicate word in the complete subject. A sentence with inverted order has one of these predicate words at the beginning of the complete subject: **an adverb, a helping verb, or a prepositional phrase.**

1. An adverb at the beginning of the sentence will modify the verb.
   (Example: Tomorrow, we / will pick apples.) (We / will pick apples tomorrow.)

2. A helping verb at the beginning of a sentence will always be part of the verb.
   (Example: Have you / ordered a dessert?) (You / have ordered a dessert.)

3. A prepositional phrase at the beginning of a sentence will often modify the verb.
   (Example: During the night, we / heard sirens.) (We / heard sirens during the night.)

To add inverted order to the Question and Answer Flow, say, "*Is this sentence in a natural or inverted order?*" If there are no predicate words in the complete subject, you say, "*Natural - No change.*" If there are predicate words at the beginning of the complete subject, you say, "*Inverted - Underline the subject parts once and the predicate parts twice.*" To identify the inverted order, draw one line under the subject parts and two lines under the predicate parts.

Reference 16: Practice Sentence

Labels:	A	Adj	Adj	SN	V	Adv	Adv
Practice:	**The**	**four**	**busy**	**workers**	**talked**	**very**	**loudly.**

Reference 17: Improved Sentence

Labels:	A	Adj	Adj	SN	V	Adv	Adv
Practice:	The	four	busy	workers	talked	very	loudly.
Improved:	**A**	**few**	**industrious**	**employees**	**conversed**	**quite**	**softly.**
	(word change)	(word change)	(synonym)	(synonym)	(synonym)	(synonym)	(antonym)

Reference 18: Subject-Verb Agreement Rules

Rule 1: A singular subject must use a singular verb form that ends in **s**: *is, was, has, does, or verbs ending with **s** or **es**.*
Rule 2: A plural subject, a compound subject, or the subject **YOU** must use a plural verb form that has **no s** ending: *are, were, do, have,* or *verbs without **s** or **es** endings.* (A plural verb form is also called the *plain form*.)

Examples: For each sentence, do these four things: 1. Write the subject. 2. Write **S** if the subject is singular or **P** if the subject is plural. 3. Write the rule number. 4. Underline the correct verb in the sentence.

Subject	S or P	Rule	
dog	S	1	1. The **dog** (chew, **chews**) on his bone.
pencil and paper	P	2	2. The **pencil** and **paper** (is, **are**) in the drawer.
You	P	2	3. **You** (**make**, makes) the bed.

Reference 19: Knowing the Difference Between Prepositions and Adverbs

Adv
In the sample sentence, *Sam ran around*, the word *around* is an adverb because it does not have a noun after it.

P   noun (OP)
In the sample sentence, *Sam ran around the track*, the word *around* is a preposition because it has the noun *track* (the object of the preposition) after it. To find the preposition and object of the preposition in the Question and Answer Flow, say: **around - P**   (Say: *around - preposition*)
     around what? track - OP   (Say: *around what? track - object of the preposition*)

Reference 20: Writing in First Person or Third Person

Events and stories can be told from different viewpoints.

First person Point of View uses the first person pronouns *I, we, me, us, my, our, mine,* and *ours* to name the speaker. If any of the first person pronouns are used in a writing, the writing is usually considered a first person writing, even though second and third person pronouns may also be used. First person shows that you (*the writer*) are speaking, and that you (*the writer*) are personally involved in what is happening.

(Examples: **I** am going fishing in **my** new boat. He likes **my** boat.)

Third person Point of View uses the third person pronouns *he, his, him, she, her, hers, it, its, they, their, theirs,* and *them* to name the person or thing spoken about. You should <u>not</u> use the first person pronouns *I, we, us, me, my, mine,* and *ours* because using the first person pronouns usually puts a writing in a first person point of view. Third person means that you (*the writer*) must write as if you are watching the events take place. Third person shows that you are writing about another person, thing, or event.

(Examples: **He** is going fishing in **his** new boat. **She** likes **his** boat.)

Reference 21: Possessive Nouns

1. A possessive noun is the name of a person, place, or thing that owns something.
2. A possessive noun will always have an apostrophe after it. It will have either an *apostrophe* before the <u>s</u> (*'s*) or an *apostrophe* after the <u>s</u> (*s'*). The apostrophe makes a noun show ownership. (*Tim's car*)
3. A possessive noun has two jobs: to show ownership or possession and to modify like an adjective.
4. When classifying a possessive noun, both jobs will be recognized by labeling it as a possessive noun adjective. Use the abbreviation **PNA** (possessive noun adjective).
5. Include possessive nouns when you are asked to identify possessive nouns or adjectives. Do not include possessive nouns when you are asked to identify regular nouns.
6. To find a possessive noun, begin with the question *whose*. (*Whose car? Tim's - PNA*)

Reference 22: Sample Paragraph in Time-Order Form

Topic: My favorite summer activities **3-points:** 1. camping   2. hiking   3. swimming

Example 1: Three-point paragraph using a standard topic sentence with non-standard points

    I enjoy three different summer activities. These summer activities are camping, hiking, and swimming. **<u>First</u>**, I enjoy camping. I like the adventure of camping in remote areas. **<u>Second</u>**, I enjoy hiking. I love discovering the hidden beauty of nature when I hike. **<u>Third</u>**, I enjoy swimming. I especially like swimming after a long hike because it is very refreshing. My three favorite summer activities provide a lot of fun for me, and they help me enjoy the outdoors.

Example 2: Three-point paragraph using a standard topic sentence with time-order points

    I enjoy three different summer activities. These summer activities are camping, hiking, and swimming. **<u>First</u>**, I enjoy camping. I like the adventure of camping in remote areas. **<u>Next</u>**, I enjoy hiking. I love discovering the hidden beauty of nature when I hike. **<u>Last</u>**, I enjoy swimming. I especially like swimming after a long hike because it is very refreshing. My three favorite summer activities provide a lot of fun for me, and they help me enjoy the outdoors.

Reference 22: Sample Paragraph in Time-Order Form, Continued

Example 3: Three-point paragraph using a general topic sentence with standard points
 	
        I enjoy participating in several summer activities. Three of these activities are camping, hiking, and swimming. <u>**My first**</u> favorite summer activity is camping. I like the adventure of camping in remote areas. <u>**My second**</u> favorite summer activity is hiking. I enjoy discovering the hidden beauty of nature when I hike. <u>**My third**</u> favorite summer activity is swimming. I especially like swimming after a long hike because it is very refreshing. My three favorite summer activities provide a lot of fun for me, and they help me enjoy the outdoors.
 	
Example 4: Three-point paragraph using a general topic sentence with time-order points
 	
        I enjoy participating in summer activities of all kinds. Three of these activities are camping, hiking, and swimming. <u>**First**</u>, I enjoy camping. I like the adventure of camping in remote areas. <u>**Next**</u>, I enjoy hiking. I enjoy discovering the hidden beauty of nature when I hike. <u>**Last**</u>, I enjoy swimming. (*or* <u>**Finally**</u>, *I enjoy swimming.*) I especially like swimming after a long hike because it is very refreshing. My three favorite summer activities provide a lot of fun for me, and they help me enjoy the outdoors.

Reference 23: Irregular Verb Chart					
PRESENT	PAST	PAST	PARTICIPLE	PRESENT	PARTICIPLE
become	became	(has)	become	(is)	becoming
blow	blew	(has)	blown	(is)	blowing
break	broke	(has)	broken	(is)	breaking
bring	brought	(has)	brought	(is)	bringing
burst	burst	(has)	burst	(is)	bursting
buy	bought	(has)	bought	(is)	buying
choose	chose	(has)	chosen	(is)	choosing
come	came	(has)	come	(is)	coming
drink	drank	(has)	drunk	(is)	drinking
drive	drove	(has)	driven	(is)	driving
eat	ate	(has)	eaten	(is)	eating
fall	fell	(has)	fallen	(is)	falling
fly	flew	(has)	flown	(is)	flying
freeze	froze	(has)	frozen	(is)	freezing
get	got	(has)	gotten	(is)	getting
give	gave	(has)	given	(is)	giving
grow	grew	(has)	grown	(is)	growing
know	knew	(has)	known	(is)	knowing
lie	lay	(has)	lain	(is)	lying
lay	laid	(has)	laid	(is)	laying
make	made	(has)	made	(is)	making
ride	rode	(has)	ridden	(is)	riding
ring	rang	(has)	rung	(is)	ringing
rise	rose	(has)	risen	(is)	rising
sell	sold	(has)	sold	(is)	selling
sing	sang	(has)	sung	(is)	singing
sink	sank	(has)	sunk	(is)	sinking
set	set	(has)	set	(is)	setting
sit	sat	(has)	sat	(is)	sitting
shoot	shot	(has)	shot	(is)	shooting
swim	swam	(has)	swum	(is)	swimming
take	took	(has)	taken	(is)	taking
tell	told	(has)	told	(is)	telling
throw	threw	(has)	thrown	(is)	throwing
wear	wore	(has)	worn	(is)	wearing
write	wrote	(has)	written	(is)	writing

Reference 24: Homonym Chart

Homonyms are words that sound the same but have different meanings and different spellings.

1. **capital** - upper part, main 2. **capitol** - statehouse	15. **lead** - metal 16. **led** - guided	29. **their** - belonging to them 30. **there** - in that place
3. **coarse** - rough 4. **course** - route	17. **no** - not so 18. **know** - to understand	31. **they're** - they are
5. **council** - assembly 6. **counsel** - advice	19. **right** - correct 20. **write** - to form letters	32. **threw** - did throw 33. **through** - from end to end
7. **forth** - forward 8. **fourth** - ordinal number	21. **principle** - a truth/rule/law 22. **principal** - chief/head person	34. **to** - toward, preposition 35. **too** - denoting excess 36. **two** - a couple
9. **its** - possessive pronoun 10. **it's** - it is	23. **stationary** - motionless 24. **stationery** - paper	37. **your** - belonging to you 38. **you're** - you are
11. **hear** - to listen 12. **here** - in this place	25. **peace** - quiet 26. **piece** - a part	39. **weak** - not strong 40. **week** - seven days
13. **knew** - understood 14. **new** - not old	27. **sent** - caused to go 28. **scent** - odor	41. **days** - more than one day 42. **daze** - a confused state

Examples: Underline the correct homonym.

1. Matthew is a member of the student (<u>**council**</u>, counsel) at school.

2. Mr. Jones (councils, <u>**counsels**</u>) the employees about their job opportunities.

Reference 25: Three-Point Paragraph and Essay

Outline of a Three-Point Paragraph

I. Title
II. Paragraph *(9 sentences)*
  A. Topic sentence
  B. A three-point sentence
  C. A **first-point** sentence
  D. A **supporting** sentence for the first point
  E. A **second-point** sentence
  F. A **supporting** sentence for the second point
  G. A **third-point** sentence
  H. A **supporting** sentence for the third point
  I. A concluding sentence

Outline of a Three-Paragraph Essay

I. Title
II. Paragraph 1 - Introduction (3 sentences)
  A. Topic and general number sentence
  B. Extra information about the topic sentence
  C. Three-point sentence
III. Paragraph 2 - Body (6-9 sentences)
  A. **First-point** sentence
  B. One or two **supporting** sentences for the first point
  C. **Second-point** sentence
  D. One or two **supporting** sentences for the second point
  E. **Third-point** sentence
  F. One or two **supporting** sentences for the third point
IV. Paragraph 3 - Conclusion (2 sentences)
  A. Concluding general statement
  B. Concluding summary sentence

Reference 26: Steps in Writing a Three-Paragraph Expository Essay

WRITING TOPIC: Stamp Collecting

LIST THE POINTS FOR THE TOPIC

♦ Select three points to list about the topic.
  1. Is inexpensive
  2. Gives sense of history
  3. Teaches one to observe

WRITING THE INTRODUCTION AND TITLE

1. Sentence #1 - Topic Sentence
   Write the topic sentence by using the words in your topic and adding a general number word, such as *several, many, some,* or *numerous,* instead of the exact number of points you will discuss.
   (Quite by accident, I discovered that, as a hobby, stamp collecting offers many rewards.)

2. Sentence #2 - Extra Information about the topic sentence
   This sentence can clarify, explain, define, or just be an extra interesting comment about the topic sentence. If you need another sentence to complete your information, write an extra sentence here. If you write an extra sentence, your introductory paragraph will have four sentences in it instead of three sentences. **(Although some of my friends collect other things, like coins and rocks, I think I like my hobby best.)**

3. Sentence #3 - Three-point sentence
   This sentence will list the three points to be discussed in the order that you will present them in the Body of your paper. You can list the points with or without the specific number in front.
   (As hobbies go, it is inexpensive, it gives one a sense of history, and it teaches one to be a careful observer.) or (My three favorite things about stamp collecting are these: it's an inexpensive hobby, it gives one a sense of history, and it teaches one to be a careful observer.)

♦ The Title - Since there are many possibilities for titles, look at the topic and the three points listed about the topic. Use some of the words in the topic and write a phrase to tell what your paragraph is about. Your title can be short or long. Capitalize the first, last, and important words in your title.
   (Why Stamp Collecting Is a Worthwhile Hobby)

WRITING THE BODY

4. Sentence #4 - First Point - Write a sentence stating your first point.
   (One of the reasons I enjoy stamp collecting is that it is inexpensive.)

5. Sentence #5 - Supporting Sentence(s) - Write one or two sentences that give more information about your first point. **(One simply has to remove the postage stamps from each day's mail.)**

6. Sentence #6 - Second Point - Write a sentence stating your second point.
   (Another reason I enjoy stamp collecting is that it gives one a sense of history.)

7. Sentence #7 - Supporting Sentence(s) - Write one or two sentences that give more information about your second point. **(Stamps feature historical figures and major events in our country's history.)**

8. Sentence #8 - Third Point - Write a sentence stating your third point.
   (I also enjoy stamp collecting because it teaches one to be a careful observer.)

9. Sentence #9 - Supporting Sentence(s) - Write one or two sentences that give more information about your third point. **(Especially with many of the older stamps, one has to look carefully at the lettering and whether the words "U.S. Postage" are located at the top or bottom of each one.)**

Reference 26: Steps in Writing a Three-Paragraph Expository Essay, Continued

WRITING THE CONCLUSION

10. <u>Sentence #10 - Concluding General Statement</u> - Read the topic sentence again and then rewrite it, using some of the same words to say the same thing in a different way.
   (To be sure, there are many advantages to stamp collecting.)

11. <u>Sentence #11 - Concluding Summary (Final) Sentence</u> - Read the three-point sentence again and then rewrite it using some of the same words to say the same thing in a different way.
   (For those who collect stamps, the hobby can be extremely rewarding in more ways than one.)

SAMPLE THREE-PARAGRAPH ESSAY

Why Stamp Collecting Is a Worthwhile Hobby

Quite by accident, I discovered that, as a hobby, stamp collecting offers many rewards. Although some of my friends collect other things, like coins and rocks, I think I like my hobby best. As hobbies go, it is inexpensive, it gives one a sense of history, and it teaches one to be a careful observer.

One of the reasons I enjoy stamp collecting is that it is inexpensive. One simply has to remove the postage stamps from each day's mail. Another reason I enjoy stamp collecting is that it gives one a sense of history. Stamps feature historical figures and major events in our country's history. I also enjoy stamp collecting because it teaches one to be a careful observer. Especially with many of the older stamps, one has to look carefully at the lettering and whether the words "U.S. Postage" are located at the top or bottom of each one.

To be sure, there are many advantages to stamp collecting. For those who collect stamps, the hobby can be extremely rewarding in more ways than one.

Reference 27: Capitalization Rules

SECTION 1: CAPITALIZE THE FIRST WORD

1. The first word of a sentence. (*He likes to take a nap.*)

2. The first word in the greeting and closing of letters. (*Dear, Yours truly*)

3. The first and last word and important words in titles of literary works.
   (*books, songs, short stories, poems, articles, movie titles, magazines*)
   (*Note: Conjunctions, articles, and prepositions with fewer than five letters are not capitalized unless they are the first or last word.*)

4. The first word of a direct quotation. (*Dad said, "We are going home."*)

5. The first word in each line of a topic outline.

SECTION 2: CAPITALIZE NAMES, INITIALS, AND TITLES OF PEOPLE

6. The pronoun I. (*May I go with you?*)

7. The names and nicknames of people. (*Sam, Joe, Jones, Slim, Shorty*)

8. Family names when used in place of or with the person's name.
   (*Grandmother, Auntie, Uncle Joe, Mother – Do NOT capitalize <u>my mother</u>.*)

9. Titles used with, or in place of, people's names.
   (*Mr., Ms., Miss, Dr. Smith, Doctor, Captain, President, Sir*)

10. People's initials. (*J.D., C. Smith*)

SECTION 3: CAPITALIZE WORDS OF TIME

11. The days of the week and months of the year. (*Monday, July*)

12. The names of holidays. (*Christmas, Thanksgiving, Easter*)

13. The names of historical events, periods, laws, documents, conflicts, and distinguished awards.
   (*Civil War, Middle Ages, Medal of Honor*)

Reference 27: Capitalization Rules, Continued

SECTION 4: CAPITALIZE NAMES OF PLACES

14. The names and abbreviations of cities, towns, counties, states, countries, and nations.
    (*Dallas, Texas, Fulton County, Africa, America, USA, AR, TX*)

15. The names of avenues, streets, roads, highways, routes, and post office boxes.
    (*Main Street, Jones Road, Highway 89, Rt. 1, Box 2, P.O. Box 45*)

16. The name of lakes, rivers, oceans, mountain ranges, deserts, parks, stars, planets, and constellations.
    (*Beaver Lake, Rocky Mountains, Venus*)

17. The names of schools and specific school courses.
    (*Walker Elementary School, Mathematics II*)

18. North, south, east, and west when they refer to sections of the country.
    (*up North, live in the East, out West*)

SECTION 5: CAPITALIZE NAMES OF OTHER NOUNS AND PROPER ADJECTIVES

19. The names of pets. (*Spot, Tweety Bird, etc.*)

20. The names of products. (*Campbell's soup, Kelly's chili, Ford cars, etc.*)

21. The names of companies, buildings, stores, ships, planes, space ships.
    (*Empire State Building, Titanic, IBM, The Big Tire Co.*)

22. Proper adjectives. (*the English language, Italian restaurant, French test*)

23. The names of clubs, organizations, or groups. (*Lion's Club, Jaycees, Beatles*)

24. The name of political parties, religious preferences, nationalities, and races.
    (*Democratic party, Republican, Jewish synagogue, American*)

Reference 28: Sentence Parts That Can Be Used for a Pattern 1 Sentence

1. Nouns

Use <u>only</u> subject nouns or object of the preposition nouns.

2. Adverbs

Tell how, when, or where.

Can be placed before or after verbs, at the beginning or end of a sentence, and in front of adjectives or other adverbs.

3. Adjectives

Tell what kind, which one, or how many.

Can be placed in front of nouns. Sometimes two or three adjectives can modify the same noun.

Articles

Adjectives that are used in front of nouns (a, an, the).

4. Verbs *Can include helping verbs.*

5. Prepositional Phrases

Can be placed before or after nouns, after verbs, adverbs, or other prepositional phrases, and at the beginning or end of a sentence.

6. Pronouns

subjective, possessive, or objective

7. Conjunctions

Connecting words for compound parts: and, or, but.

8. Interjections

Usually found at the beginning of a sentence. Can show strong or mild emotion.

Reference 29A: Punctuation Rules

SECTION 6: END MARK PUNCTUATION

1. Use a (.) for the end punctuation of a sentence that makes a statement.
   (*Mom baked us a cake.*)
2. Use a (?) for the end punctuation of a sentence that asks a question.
   (*Are you going to town?*)
3. Use an (!) for the end punctuation of a sentence that expresses strong feeling.
   (*That bee stung me!*)
4. Use a (.) for the end punctuation of a sentence that gives a command or makes a request.
   (*Close the door.*)

SECTION 7: COMMAS TO SEPARATE TIME WORDS

5. Use a comma between the day of the week and the month. (*Friday, July 23*)
   Use a comma between the day and year. (*July 23, 2009*)
6. Use a comma to separate the year from the rest of the sentence when the year follows the month or the month and the day.
   (*We spent May, 2001, with Mom. We spent July 23, 2001, with Dad.*)

SECTION 8: COMMAS TO SEPARATE PLACE WORDS

7. Use a comma to separate the city from the state or country.
   (*I will go to Dallas, Texas. He is from Paris, France.*)
8. Use a comma to separate the state or country from the rest of the sentence when the name of the state or country follows the name of a city.
   (*We flew to Dallas, Texas, in June. We flew to Paris, France, in July.*)

SECTION 9: COMMAS TO MAKE MEANINGS CLEAR

9. Use a comma to separate words or phrases in a series.
   (*We had soup, crackers, and milk.*)
10. Use commas to separate introductory words such as *Yes, Well, Oh,* and *No* from the rest of a sentence.
    (*Oh, I didn't know that.*)
11. Use commas to set off most appositives. An appositive is a word, phrase, title, or degree used directly after another word or name to explain it or to rename it.
    (*Sue, the girl next door, likes to draw.*)
    One-word appositives can be written two different ways: *(1) My brother, Tim, is riding in the horse show.*
    (2) My brother Tim is riding in the horse show. Your assignments will require one-word appositives to be set off with commas.
12. Use commas to separate a noun of direct address (the name of a person directly spoken to) from the rest of the sentence. (*Mom, do I really have to go?*)

SECTION 10: PUNCTUATION IN GREETINGS AND CLOSINGS OF LETTERS

13. Use a comma (,) after the salutation (greeting) of a friendly letter. (*Dear Sam,*)
14. Use a comma (,) after the closing of any letter. (*Yours truly,*)
15. Use a colon (:) after the salutation (greeting) of a business letter. (*Dear Sir:*)

Reference 29B: Punctuation Rules

SECTION 11: PERIODS

16. Use a period after most abbreviations or titles that are accepted in formal writing.
(*Mr., Ms., Dr., Capt., St., Ave., St. Louis*) (*Note: These abbreviations cannot be used by themselves. They must always be used with a proper noun.*)

    In the abbreviations of many well-known organizations or words, periods are not required. (*USA, GM, TWA, GTE, AT&T, TV, AM, FM, GI, etc.*) Use only one period after an abbreviation at the end of a statement. Do not put an extra period for the end mark punctuation.

17. Use a period after initials. (*C. Smith, D.J. Brewton, Thomas A. Jones*)

18. Place a period after Roman numerals, Arabic numbers, and letters of the alphabet in an outline.
(*II., IV., 5., 25., A., B.*)

SECTION 12: APOSTROPHES

19. Form a contraction by using an apostrophe in place of a letter or letters that have been left out.
(*I'll, he's, isn't, wasn't, can't*)

20. Form the possessive of singular and plural nouns by using an apostrophe.
(*boy's ball, boys' ball, children's ball*)

21. Form the plurals of letters, symbols, numbers, and signs with the apostrophe plus *s* (*'s*). (*9's, B's, b's*)

SECTION 13: UNDERLINING

22. Use underlining or italics for titles of books, magazines, works of art, ships, newspapers, motion pictures, etc. (*A famous movie is <u>Gone With the Wind</u>. Our newspaper is the <u>Cabot Star Herald</u>.*) (<u>*Titanic*</u>, <u>*Charlotte's Web*</u>, etc.)

SECTION 14: QUOTATION MARKS

23. Use quotation marks to set off the titles of songs, short stories, short poems, articles, essays, short plays, and book chapters. (*Do you like to sing the song "America" in music class?*)

24. Quotation marks are used at the beginning and end of the person's words to separate what the person actually said from the rest of the sentence. Since the quotation tells what is being said, it will always have quotation marks around it.

25. The words that tell who is speaking are the explanatory words. Do not set explanatory words off with quotation marks. (*Fred said, "I'm here."*) (**Fred said** *is explanatory and should not be set off with quotations.*)

26. A new paragraph is used to indicate a change of speaker.

27. When a speaker's speech is longer than one paragraph, quotation marks are used at the beginning of each paragraph and at the end of the last paragraph of that speaker's speech.

28. Use single quotation marks to enclose a quotation within a quotation.
(*"My teddy bear says 'I love you' four different ways," said little Amy.*)

29. Use a period at the end of explanatory words that come at the end of a sentence.

30. Use a comma to separate a direct quotation from the explanatory words.

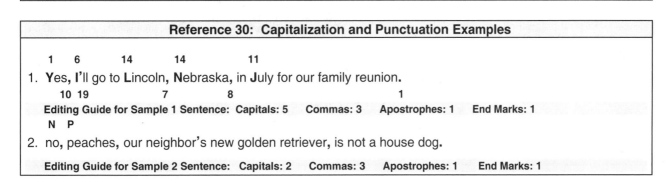

Reference 30: Capitalization and Punctuation Examples

 1   6   14   14   11

1. Yes, I'll go to Lincoln, Nebraska, in July for our family reunion.
    10 19   7   8   1

   Editing Guide for Sample 1 Sentence: Capitals: 5   Commas: 3   Apostrophes: 1   End Marks: 1
   N P

2. no, peaches, our neighbor's new golden retriever, is not a house dog.

   Editing Guide for Sample 2 Sentence: Capitals: 2   Commas: 3   Apostrophes: 1   End Marks: 1

Reference 31: Three- Paragraph Essay and Five-Paragraph Essay

Outline of a 3-Paragraph Essay	Outline of a 5-Paragraph Essay
I. Title	I. Title
II. Paragraph 1 - Introduction (3 sentences) 　　A. Topic and general number sentence 　　B. Extra information about the topic sentence 　　C. Three-point sentence	II. Paragraph 1 - Introduction　　(3 sentences) 　　A. Topic and general number sentence 　　B. Extra information about the topic sentence 　　C. Three-point sentence
III. Paragraph 2 - Body　　(6-9 sentences) 　　A. **First-point** sentence 　　B. One or two **supporting** sentences 　　　　for the first point 　　C. **Second-point** sentence 　　D. One or two **supporting** sentence 　　　　for the second point 　　E. **Third-point** sentence 　　F. One or two **supporting** sentences 　　　　for the third point	III. Paragraph 2 - First Point Body　　(3-4 sentences) 　　A. **First-point** sentence 　　B. Two or three **supporting** sentences for the first point
	IV. Paragraph 3 - Second Point Body　(3-4 sentences) 　　A. **Second-point** sentence 　　B. Two or three **supporting** sentences for the second point
	V. Paragraph 4 - Third Point Body　　(3-4 sentences) 　　A. **Third-point** sentence 　　B. Two or three **supporting** sentences for the third point
IV. Paragraph 3 - Conclusion (2 sentences) 　　A. Concluding general statement 　　B. Concluding summary sentence	VI. Paragraph 5 - Conclusion　　(2 sentences) 　　A. Concluding general statement 　　　　(Restatement of the topic sentence) 　　B. Concluding summary sentence 　　　　(Restatement of the enumeration sentence)

Reference 32: This reference is located on pages 25 & 26.

Reference 33: This reference is located on page 27.

Reference 34: Direct Object, Verb-transitive, and Pattern 2

1. A **direct object** is a noun or pronoun after the verb that completes the meaning of the sentence.

2. A **direct object** is labeled as **DO**.

3. To find the **direct object**, ask WHAT or WHOM after the verb.

4. A **direct object** must be verified to mean someone or something different from the subject noun.

5. A **verb-transitive** is an action verb with a direct object after it and is labeled **V-t**. (Whatever receives the action of a transitive verb is the direct object.)

Sample Sentence for the exact words to say to find the direct object and transitive verb.

1. Larry rides a mule.
2. Who rides a mule? Larry - SN
3. What is being said about Larry? Larry rides - V
4. Larry rides what? mule - verify the noun
5. Does mule mean the same thing as Larry? No.
6. Mule - DO *(Say: mule - direct object.)*
7. Rides - V-t *(Say: rides - verb-transitive.)*
8. A - A

9. SN V-t DO P2 Check
    (Say: Subject Noun, Verb-transitive, Direct Object, Pattern 2, Check.)
    (This first check is to make sure the "t" is added to the verb.)
10. Verb-transitive - check again.
    ("Check again" means to check for prepositional phrases and then go through the rest of the Question and Answer Flow.)
11. No prepositional phrases.
12. Period, statement, declarative sentence.
13. Go back to the verb - divide the complete subject from the complete predicate.
14. Is there an adverb exception? No.
15. Is this sentence in a natural or inverted order? Natural - no change.

Reference 32: Steps in Writing a Five-Paragraph Expository Essay

WRITING TOPIC: Stamp Collecting

THREE MAIN POINTS

♦ Select the points to list about the topic.
    1. **Is inexpensive**
    2. **Gives sense of history**
    3. **Teaches one to observe**

WRITING THE INTRODUCTION AND TITLE

1. Sentence #1 - Topic Sentence
   Write the topic sentence by using the words in your topic and adding a general number word, such as *several, many, some*, or *numerous*, instead of the exact number of points you will discuss.
   (Quite by accident, I discovered that, as a hobby, stamp collecting offers many rewards.)

2. Sentence #2 - Extra Information about the topic sentence
   This sentence can clarify, explain, define, or just be an extra interesting comment about the topic sentence. If you need another sentence to complete your information, write an extra sentence here. If you write an extra sentence, your introductory paragraph will have four sentences in it instead of three and that is okay.
   (Although some of my friends collect other things, like coins and rocks, I think I like my hobby best.)

3. Sentence #3 - Three-point sentence
   This sentence will list the three points to be discussed in the order that you will present them in the body of your paper. You can list the points with or without the specific number in front.
   (As hobbies go, it is inexpensive, it gives one a sense of history, and it teaches one to be a careful observer.) or (My three favorite things about stamp collecting are these: it's an inexpensive hobby, it gives one a sense of history, and it teaches one to observe.)

♦ The Title - Since there are many possibilities for titles, look at the topic and the three points listed about the topic. Use some of the words in the topic and write a phrase to tell what your paragraph is about. Your title can be short or long. Capitalize the first, last, and important words in your title.
   (Why Stamp Collecting Is a Worthwhile Hobby)

WRITING THE BODY

4. Sentence #4 - First Point - Write a sentence stating your first point.
   (One of the reasons I enjoy stamp collecting is that it is inexpensive.)

5. Sentences #5 - #7 - Supporting Sentences - Write two or three sentences that give more information about your first point.
   (For one thing, rather than having to buy new stamps, one simply has to remove the postage stamps from each day's mail.) (Other than the cost of an album, which is nominal, and a package of gummed hinges for mounting, there are no other expenses.) (To be sure, one can collect stamps and not go broke.)

6. Sentence #8 - Second Point - Write a sentence stating your second point.
   (Another reason I enjoy stamp collecting is that it gives one a sense of history.)

7. Sentences #9 - #11 - Supporting Sentences - Write two or three sentences that give more information about your second point.
   (For example, stamps feature historical figures in our country's history – people like presidents, inventors, scientists, and authors of all types.) (They also feature major events in our nation's past – events such as natural disasters, wars, treaties, and various "firsts" in the fields of transportation and communication.) (Stamp collecting, as one can see, is a means of gaining perspective on what brought us as a nation to where we are today.)

Reference 32: Steps in Writing a Five-Paragraph Expository Essay, Continued

8. Sentence #12 - Third Point - Write a sentence stating your third point.
   (I also enjoy stamp collecting because it teaches one to be a careful observer.)

9. Sentences #13 - #15 - Supporting Sentences - Write two or three sentences that give more information about your third point.
   (In order to place stamps properly on the pages of an album, one has to be sure the lettering corresponds – same style, same size, and same location.) (Besides that, one has to note whether the words "U. S. Postage" are located at the top or bottom of each stamp.) (Particularly with the early stamps, whose coloring in the various series remained the same, one has to observe the wording and its placement very carefully in order to place the stamps properly in the album.)

WRITING THE CONCLUSION

10. Sentence #16 - Concluding General Statement - Read the topic sentence again and then rewrite it using some of the same words to say the same thing in a different way.
    (To be sure, there are many advantages to stamp collecting.)

11. Sentence #17 - Concluding Summary Sentence - Read the three-point sentence again and then rewrite it, using some of the same words to say the same thing in a different way.
    (For those who collect stamps, the hobby can be extremely rewarding in more ways than one.)

SAMPLE FIVE-PARAGRAPH ESSAY

Why Stamp Collecting Is a Worthwhile Hobby

Quite by accident, I discovered that, as a hobby, stamp collecting offers many rewards. Although some of my friends collect other things, like coins and rocks, I think I like my hobby best. As hobbies go, it is inexpensive, it gives one a sense of history, and it teaches one to be a careful observer.

One of the reasons that I enjoy stamp collecting is that it is inexpensive. For one thing, rather than having to buy new stamps, one simply has to remove the postage stamps from each day's mail. Other than the cost of an album, which is nominal, and a package of gummed hinges for mounting, there are no other expenses. To be sure, one can collect stamps and not go broke.

Another reason I enjoy stamp collecting is that it gives one a sense of history. For example, stamps feature historical figures in our country's history – people like presidents, inventors, scientists, and authors of all types. They also feature major events in our nation's past – events such as natural disasters, wars, treaties, and various "firsts" in the fields of transportation and communication. Stamp collecting, as one can see, is a means of gaining perspective on what brought us as a nation to where we are today.

I also enjoy stamp collecting because it teaches one to be a careful observer. In order to place stamps properly on the pages of an album, one has to be sure the lettering corresponds – same style, same size, and same location. Besides that, one has to note whether the words "U.S. Postage" are located at the top or bottom of each stamp. Particularly with the early stamps, whose coloring in the various series remained the same, one has to observe the wording and its placement very carefully in order to place the stamps properly in the album.

To be sure, there are many advantages to stamp collecting. For those who collect stamps, the hobby can be extremely rewarding in more ways than one.

Reference 33: Persuasive Paragraph and Essay Guidelines

Guidelines for a Persuasive Paragraph	Guidelines for a 3-Paragraph Persuasive Essay
Paragraph (10-13 sentences)	1. Paragraph 1 – Introduction (3 sentences)
A. **Topic** sentence (opinion statement)	A. **Topic** sentence (opinion statement)
B. **General number** sentence	B. **Reason** sentence
C. **First-point** persuasive sentence	C. **General number** sentence
D. 1 or 2 **supporting** sentences for the first point	2. Paragraph 2 – Body (6-9 sentences)
E. **Second-point** persuasive sentence	A. **First-point** persuasive sentence
F. 1 or 2 **supporting** sentences for the second point	B. 1 or 2 **supporting** sentences for the first point
G. **Third-point** persuasive sentence	C. **Second-point** persuasive sentence
H. 1 or 2 **supporting** sentences for the third point	D. 1 or 2 **supporting** sentences for the second point
I. **In conclusion** sentence (Repeat topic idea)	E. **Third-point** persuasive sentence
J. **Final summary** sentence (Summarize reasons)	F. 1 or 2 **supporting** sentences for the third point
	3. Paragraph 3 - Conclusion (2 sentences)
	A. **In conclusion** sentence (Repeat topic idea)
	B. **Final summary** sentence (Summarize reasons)

Need for Biking Trails

Every town needs biking trails. They would provide safety for children who especially enjoy riding bikes, either alone or with their friends. There are some obvious safety benefits for bikers and non-bikers that would come from biking trails.

One of the obvious benefits of a biking trail is that it would keep children off the streets. Since streets are heavily traveled, biking trails would lessen the risk of bicycle accidents. Another benefit of a biking trail is that it would free the sidewalks for pedestrian traffic. In most instances, sidewalks will not accommodate both bikers and walkers without someone being hurt or inconvenienced. A third reason for a biking trail is that it would give bikers better exposure to the outdoors. Bikers could enjoy the luxuries of wildflowers and wildlife of various types on a biking trail and without the impediments of intersections and stop signs.

In conclusion, in every community, the young and old alike would benefit from a biking trail. A biking trail would increase the security and pleasure of bikers, walkers, and drivers alike.

Reference 35: Regular Editing Checklist

Read each sentence and go through the Sentence Checkpoints below.

_____ E1. Sentence sense check. (Check for words left out or words repeated.)

_____ E2. First word, capital letter check. End mark check. Any other capitalization check. Any other punctuation check.

_____ E3. Sentence structure and punctuation check. (Check for correct construction and correct punctuation of a simple sentence, a simple sentence with compound parts, a compound sentence, or a complex sentence.)

_____ E4. Spelling and homonym check. (Check for misspelled words and incorrect homonym choices.)

_____ E5. Usage check. (Check subject-verb agreement, a/an choice, pronoun/antecedent agreement, pronoun cases, degrees of adjectives, double negatives, verb tenses, and contractions.)

Read each paragraph and go through the Paragraph Checkpoints below.

_____ E6. Check to see that each paragraph is indented.

_____ E7. Check each paragraph for a topic sentence.

_____ E8. Check each sentence to make sure it supports the topic of the paragraph.

_____ E9. Check the content for interest and creativity. Do not begin all sentences with the same word, and use a variety of simple, compound, and complex sentences.

_____ E10. Check the type and format of the writing assigned.

Reference 36: Editing Example

Topic: Application of theater skills
Three main points: **(1. Speak clearly   2. Speak extemporaneously   3. Exhibit poise)**

Major
Reasons to major in Theater

→   **a**   **there**
Being a theater major can teach an person a number of invaluable lessons. Although their may
                              (,)
be few opportunities to act professionally one can take the performing skills and apply them in other
     (.)T   **(,)**
professions three important lessons one can apply in a host of professions are speaking clearly
                (,)
speaking extemporaneously and exhibiting poise.
One→
one of the important application skills of a theater major is the art of speaking clearly. Proper
                      not   **a**
enunciation of words knot only makes for effective communication, but it also creates an positive
  A   **who**
impression on others. another of the application skills is that of impromptu speaking. People whom
                clearly   **always**   **an**
are able to think quickly and clear can almost alway convince others to their way of thinking; they exude a
                                                  is
unmistakable confidence in their use of language. Another application of theater skills are exhibiting poise
                        Their
in front of a group of people. There "stage presence" enables them to carry on.
      conclusion   **to**
   In Conclusion, a host of theater skills can be applied too many different professions. To be able to
                                    to
speak clearly and without preparation and with poise are keys too success in any walk of life.

Total Mistakes: 23
Editing Guide: Sentence checkpoints: **E1, E2, E3, E4, E5**   Paragraph checkpoints: **E6, E7, E8, E9, E10**

Reference 37: Complete Sentences and Sentence Fragments

Part 1

Identifying simple sentences and fragments: Write **S** for a complete sentence and **F** for a sentence fragment on the line beside each group of words below.

F	1.	The huge mountains in the distance.
S	2.	Babies squealed.
F	3.	For the biggest prize.
F	4.	Scaling the steepest cliffs.
S	5.	Life preservers are essential.

Part 2

Fragment Examples: (1) falling down the steps (2) the funny monkeys at the zoo (3) as I talked to my mom
                             (4) for a bottle of milk

Part 3

Directions: Add the part that is underlined in parentheses to make each fragment into a complete sentence.

1. On the edge of the diving board for a brief moment. (subject part, predicate part, <u>both the subject and predicate</u>)
   (**The first diver poised** on the edge of the diving board for a brief moment.)

2. The excited fans. (subject part, <u>predicate part</u>, both the subject and predicate)
   (The excited fans **clapped and yelled loudly for the players.**)

3. Was rolling down the hill. (<u>subject part</u>, predicate part, both the subject and predicate)
   (**My expensive camera** was rolling down the hill.)

Reference 38: Simple Sentences, Compound Parts, and Fragments

Example 1: The little girl looked shyly at her teacher. (**S**)
Example 2: Carla's <u>mom and dad</u> attended her graduation. (**SCS**)
Example 3: Jennifer <u>jumped and twirled</u> during the dance rehearsal. (**SCV**)

Part 2: Identify each kind of sentence by writing the abbreviation in the blank. (**S, SS, F, SCS, SCV**)

SCV	1. The children ran and shouted during recess.
SCS	2. The rain and sleet fell steadily.
F	3. During the picnic at noon in the park.
S	4. Our electricity went off during the ice storm.
SS	5. I watched a movie. It was good.

Part 3: Put a slash to separate each run-on sentence below. Then, correct the run-on sentences by rewriting them as indicated by the labels in parentheses at the end of each sentence.

1. The wasps were swarming **/** they were upset. (**SS**)
   The wasps were swarming. They were upset.
2. The horse is in the barn **/** the cow is in the barn. (**SCS**)
   The horse and cow are in the barn.
3. The ambulance parked **/** it waited for a call. (**SCV**)
   The ambulance parked and waited for a call.

Reference 39: The Compound Sentence

1. Compound means two. A compound sentence is two complete sentences joined together correctly.

2. <u>The first way to join two sentences</u> to make a compound sentence is to <u>use a comma and a conjunction.</u> The formula for you to follow will always be given at the end of the sentence. The formula gives the abbreviation for "compound sentence" and lists the conjunction to use (**CD, but**). Remember to place the comma BEFORE the conjunction.
   Example: She studied for her driver's **test, but** she did not pass it. (CD, but)

3. <u>The second way to join two sentences</u> and make a compound sentence is to <u>use a semicolon and a connective (conjunctive) adverb.</u> The formula to follow is given at the end of the sentence. The formula gives the abbreviation for "compound sentence" and lists the connective adverb to use (**CD; however,**). Remember to place a semicolon BEFORE the connective adverb and a comma AFTER the connective adverb. **Example:** She studied for her driver's test**; however,** she did not pass it. (CD; however,)

4. <u>The third way to join two sentences</u> and make a compound sentence is to <u>use a semicolon only.</u> The formula to follow is given at the end of the sentence and lists the semicolon after the abbreviation for "compound sentence" (**CD;**). Remember, there is no conjunction or connective adverb when the semicolon is used alone. **Example:** She studied for her driver's **test; she** did not pass it. (CD;)

5. Compound sentences should be closely related in thought and importance.
   <u>Correct:</u>   She studied for her driver's **test, but** she did not pass it.
   <u>Incorrect:</u> She studied for her driver's test, but she preferred toast.

Reference 40: Coordinate Conjunction and Connective Adverb Chart

Type of Conj / Adv	More Information	Contrast/Choice	Alternative	As a result
Coordinate Conjunction	,and ,nor	,but ,yet	,or	,so (as a result) so (that) - no comma
Connective Adverbs	;moreover, ;furthermore, ;besides, ;also, ;likewise,	;however, ;nevertheless,	;otherwise,	;therefore, ;hence, ;thus, ;consequently, ;accordingly,

Reference 41: Examples Using S, SCS, SCV, and CD to Correct Run-On Sentences

Put a slash to separate the two complete thoughts in each run-on sentence. Correct the run-on sentences or fragments as indicated by the labels in parentheses at the end of each sentence.

1. Dave plans to move / he doesn't like packing. (**CD**, but)
   Dave plans to move, but he doesn't like packing.

2. George will drive to Denver / there is a snow advisory posted. (**CD**; however,)
   George will drive to Denver; however, there is a snow advisory posted.

3. I always climb the flights of stairs / the exercise is healthy. (**CD**;)
   I always climb the flights of stairs; the exercise is healthy.

4. Kimberly gathered daisies along the roadside / Kimberly gathered rocks along the roadside. (**S**)
   Kimberly gathered daisies and rocks along the roadside. *(Simple sentences can have other compound parts.)*

5. Larry woke at 6:00 / Sue woke at 6:00. (**SCS**)
   Larry and Sue woke at 6:00.

6. For recreation, Judy plays the piano / she writes songs. (**SCV**)
   For recreation, Judy plays the piano and writes songs.

Reference 42: Identifying S, F, SCS, SCV, and CD

Part 1: Identify each kind of sentence by writing the abbreviation in the blank (**S**, **F**, **SCS**, **SCV**, **CD**).

CD	1.	Jeff did not study last night; therefore, he is in a panic now.
F	2.	Beside a creek where a grove of trees stood.
SCV	3.	We flew into Chicago and took a taxi to the stadium.
S	4.	After school, Josh mows yards three nights a week.
SCS	5.	The superintendent and principal met behind closed doors.
CD	6.	Rhonda wrapped the presents, and she took them to her mother's.

Part 2: On your paper, use the ways listed below to correct this run-on sentence: **The vase cracked it did not break.**

7. CD, but   **The vase cracked, but it did not break.**   8. SCV   **The vase cracked but did not break.**

Reference 43: This reference is located on page 32.

Reference 44: Examples of Complex Sentences

Part 1: Put a slash to separate each sentence. Rewrite and correct the run-on sentences as indicated by the labels in parentheses.	**Part 2:** Identify each kind of sentence by writing the abbreviation in the blank (**S**, **F**, **SCS**, **SCV**, **CD**, **CX**).
1. Larry fell down / he broke his arm. (**CX**, when 1) 2. He overslept / he was late for work. (**CX**, because 1) 3. You will not graduate / you do not study. (**CX**, if 2) 4. The phone rang / I burned my finger. (**CX**, before 1)	5. S After midnight, the tornado warning sirens blared. 6. CX As he left, he threw us a kiss. 7. SCV My tutor broke her arm and quit. 8. SCS Tomorrow, you and the other team captain will lead the parade.
Key for 1-4: 1. **When Larry fell down, he broke his arm.** 3. **You will not graduate if you do not study.**	2. **Because he overslept, he was late for work.** 4. **Before the phone rang, I burned my finger.**

Reference 43: The Complex Sentence and Subordinate Conjunctions

Definition: A complex sentence is made by correctly joining two sentences: an independent sentence and a subordinate sentence.

1. **Independent sentence:** He won the spelling bee.
2. **Subordinate sentence:** <u>After</u> he won the spelling bee.
3. **Complex sentence:**   <u>After</u> he won the spelling bee, <u>he earned the respect of his classmates.</u>

Example 1: he won the spelling bee he earned the respect of his classmates. (CX, after 1)
After he won the spelling bee, he earned the respect of his classmates.

Example 2: he earned the respect of his classmates he won the spelling bee. (CX, after 2)
He earned the respect of his classmates after he won the spelling bee.

Example 3: **After he won the spelling bee,** he earned the respect of his classmates.

Example 4: He earned the respect of his classmates **after he won the spelling bee**.

Review

A. A sentence becomes a complex sentence when you add a subordinate conjunction to one of the two sentences that make up a complex sentence.
B. Any independent sentence can be made subordinate (dependent) by simply adding a subordinate conjunction to the beginning of that sentence.

   Subordinate sentences: (**After** he won) (**When** he won) (**Because** he won) (**Until** he won)

A LIST OF THE MOST COMMON SUBORDINATE CONJUNCTIONS

A subordinate conjunction is a conjunction that always introduces a subordinate sentence. Since there are many subordinate conjunctions, only a few of the most common subordinate conjunctions are provided in the list below.

after	*because*	*except*	*so that*	*though*	*when*
although	*before*	*if*	*than*	*unless*	*where*
as, or *as soon as*	*even though*	*since*	*that*	*until*	*while*

Reference 45: Making Nouns Possessive

1. For a singular noun - add (**'s**)	2. For a plural noun that ends in *s* - add (**'**)	3. For a plural noun that does not end in *s* - add (**'s**)
Rule 1: boy's	**Rule 2: boys'**	**Rule 3: men's**

Part A: Underline each noun to be made possessive and write singular or plural (**S-P**), the rule number, and the possessive form. Part B: Write each noun as singular possessive and then as plural possessive.

Part A	S-P	Rule	Possessive Form	Part B	Singular Poss	Plural Poss
1. <u>oyster</u> pearl	S	1	**oyster's pearl**	5. class	**class's**	**classes'**
2. <u>ducks</u> feathers	P	2	**ducks' feathers**	6. child	**child's**	**children's**
3. <u>baboon</u> grin	S	1	**baboon's grin**	7. roof	**roof's**	**roofs'**
4. <u>kittens</u> cries	P	2	**kittens' cries**	8. Jones	**Jones's**	**Jones' or Joneses'**

Reference 46: Indirect Object and Pattern 3

1. An **indirect object** is a noun or pronoun.
2. An **indirect object** receives what the direct object names.
3. An **indirect object** is located between the verb-transitive and the direct object.
4. An **indirect object** is labeled as **IO**.
5. To find the **indirect object**, ask TO WHOM or FOR WHOM after the direct object.

Sample Sentence for the exact words to say to find the indirect object.

1. Chris sang her a lullaby.
2. Who sang her a lullaby? Chris - SN
3. What is being said about Chris? Chris sang - V
4. Chris sang what? lullaby - verify the noun
5. Does lullaby mean the same thing as Chris? No.
6. Lullaby - DO
7. Sang - V-t
8. Chris sang lullaby for whom? her - IO
   (*Say: her - indirect object.*)
9. A - A

10. SN V-t IO DO P3 Check
    (*Say: Subject Noun, Verb-transitive, Indirect Object, Direct Object, Pattern 3, Check.*) (*This first check is to make sure the "t" is added to the verb.*)
11. Verb-transitive - check again.
    (*"Check again" means to check for prepositional phrases and then go through the rest of the Question and Answer Flow.*)
12. No prepositional phrases.
13. Period, statement, declarative sentence
14. Go back to the verb - divide the complete subject from the complete predicate.
15. Is there an adverb exception? No.
16. Is this sentence in a natural or inverted order? Natural - no change.

Reference 47: Subjective, Objective, and Possessive Pronoun Cases

1. The **subject** pronouns are in the **subjective case:** *I, we, he, she, it, they,* and *you.*
   Use subjective case pronouns for subjects or predicate pronouns.
2. The **object** pronouns are in the **objective case:** *me, us, him, her, it, them,* and *you.*
   Use objective case pronouns for objects: object of a preposition, direct object, or indirect object.
3. The **possessive** pronouns are in the **possessive case:** *my, our, his, her, its, their, your,* and *mine.*
   Use possessive case pronouns to show ownership.

Practice Section: For Sentences 1-4, replace each underlined pronoun by writing the correct form in the first blank and **S** or **O** for **S**ubjective or **O**bjective case in the second blank.

1. Molly and <u>me</u> are waiting on Tim.   <u>I</u> <u>S</u>
2. Dad wants to invite Howard and <u>they</u>.   <u>them</u> <u>O</u>
3. Do you want <u>she</u> and <u>I</u> to choose? <u>her and me</u> <u>O</u>
4. Did you speak to <u>he</u> or <u>I</u>? <u>him or me</u> <u>O</u>

Reference 48: Quotation Rules for Beginning Quotes

1. **Pattern:** "C -quote- (,!?) " <u>explanatory words</u> (.)
   (Quotation marks, capital letter, quote, end punctuation choice, quotation marks closed, explanatory words, period)
2. Underline **end explanatory words** and use a period at the end.
3. You should see the **beginning quote** – Use quotation marks at the beginning and end of what is said. Then, put a comma, question mark, or exclamation point (no period) after the quote but in front of the quotation mark.
4. **Capitalize** the beginning of a quote and any proper nouns or the pronoun *I*.
5. **Punctuate** the rest of the sentence by checking for any apostrophes, periods, or commas that may be needed within the sentence.

Guided Practice

Sentence: the poets and i are reading poetry on tuesday with m k miller the director said

1. Pattern: "C -quote- (,!?) " <u>explanatory words</u> (.)
2. the poets and i are reading poetry on tuesday with m k miller **<u>the director said</u>**(.)
3. "the poets and i are reading poetry on tuesday with m k miller**,**" <u>the director said</u>.
4. "**T**he poets and **I** are reading poetry on **T**uesday with **M K M**iller," <u>the director said</u>.
5. "The poets and I are reading poetry on Tuesday with M**.** K**.** Miller," <u>the director said</u>.
6. **Corrected Sentence:** "The poets and I are reading poetry on Tuesday with M. K. Miller," the director said.

Reference 49: Quotation Rules for End Quotes

1. **Pattern:** <u>C –explanatory words</u>(,) "C -quote- (.!?) "
   (Capital letter, explanatory words, comma, quotation marks, capital letter, quote, end punctuation choice, quotation marks closed)
2. Underline **beginning explanatory words** and use a comma after them.
3. You should see the **end quote** – Use quotation marks at the beginning and end of what is said. Then, put a period, question mark, or exclamation point (no comma) after the quote, usually in front of the quotation mark.
4. **Capitalize** the first of the explanatory words at the beginning of a sentence, the beginning of the quote, and any proper nouns or the pronoun *I*.
5. **Punctuate** the rest of the sentence by checking for any apostrophes, periods, or commas that may be needed within the sentence.

Guided Practice

Sentence: the director said the poets and i are reading poetry on tuesday with m k miller

1. Pattern: <u>C -explanatory words</u>(,) "C -quote- (.!?) "
2. **<u>the director said</u>**(,) the poets and i are reading poetry on tuesday with m k miller
3. <u>the director said</u>, "the poets and i are reading poetry on tuesday with m k miller**. "**
4. <u>The director said</u>, "**T**he poets and **I** are reading poetry on **T**uesday with **M K M**iller."
5. <u>The director said</u>, "The poets and I are reading poetry on Tuesday with M**.** K**.** Miller."
6. **Corrected Sentence:** The director said, "The poets and I are reading poetry on Tuesday with M. K. Miller."

Reference 50: Quotation Rules for Split Quotes

1. **Pattern:** "**C** -quote- **(,)** "**c** -explanatory words**(,)** "**c** -quote- **(.!?)** "
   (Quotation marks, capital letter, first part of quote, comma, quotation marks, explanatory words, comma, quotation marks again, second part of quote, end punctuation choice, quotation marks.)

2. Underline **middle explanatory words** and use a comma after them.

3. You should see the **first part of a split quote** - Use quotation marks at the beginning and end of the first part of what is said. Then, put a comma after the first part of the quote but in front of the quotation mark.

4. You should see the **second part of a split quote** - Use quotation marks at the beginning and end of the second part of what is said. Then, put end mark punctuation (no comma) after the quote but usually in front of the quotation mark.

5. **Capitalize** the beginning of a quote and any proper nouns or the pronoun *I*. (Do not capitalize the first word of the second part unless it is a proper noun or the pronoun *I*.)

6. **Punctuate** the rest of the sentence by checking for any apostrophes, periods, or commas that may be needed within the sentence.

Guided Practice

Sentence: the poets and i the director said are reading poetry on tuesday with m k miller

1. Pattern: "**C** -quote- **(,)** "**c** -explanatory words**(,)** "**c** -quote- **(.!?)** "
2. the poets and i **the director said(,)** are reading poetry on tuesday with m k miller
3. "the poets and i**,**" the director said, are reading poetry on tuesday with m k miller
4. "the poets and i," the director said, "are reading poetry on tuesday with m k miller**(.)**"
5. "**T**he poets and **I**," the director said, "are reading poetry on **T**uesday with **M K M**iller."
6. "The poets and I," the director said, "are reading poetry on Tuesday with M. K. Miller."
7. **Corrected Sentence:** "The poets and I," the director said, "are reading poetry on Tuesday with M. K. Miller."

Note: When you enclose two sentences in quotation marks, you still have two sentences, not a split quote. "The poets and I are reading poetry on Tuesday," the director said. "I think they need the experience."

Reference 51: Other Quotation Rules

1. Longer Quotes

   A. When a quotation consists of several sentences, put quotation marks only at the beginning and at the end of the whole quotation, not around each sentence in the quotation.

      Cathy repeated, "I do not work on Fridays. If you want to go shopping then, I'll be available."

   B. When one person has a lengthy quote which is longer than one paragraph, quotation marks are used at the beginning of each paragraph and at the end of the last paragraph of that speaker's quote. Then, when the speaker changes, a new paragraph is started.

      "_____

      _____ (same speaker continues)

      "_____

      _____" (same speaker ends)

      "_____" (new speaker begins and ends)

2. A Quote Within a Quote

Single quotation marks are used to punctuate a quotation within a quotation.

      "Did she say, 'Scotland is my homeland'?" Charlie asked.

3. Quotation Marks to Punctuate Titles

Quotation marks are used to punctuate titles of songs, poems, short stories, chapters of books, articles, TV programs, and short plays. (*Capitalize the first word, last word, and every word except for articles, short prepositions, and short conjunctions.*)

      Her favorite poem is "Two Tramps in Mud Time."

4. Direct Quotations, Indirect Quotations, and Statements

   A. A direct quotation occurs when you show exactly what someone says by using quotation marks.

      Direct quotation: Al said yesterday, "I'd like to buy a ranch."

   B. An indirect quotation occurs when you simply describe what someone says without using his exact words.

      Indirect quotation: Al said he would like to buy a ranch.

   C. A statement occurs when no speaker is mentioned and no quotation is used.

      Statement: Al would like to buy a ranch.

Reference 52: This reference is located on page 37.

Reference 53: Regular and Irregular Verbs

Most verbs are **regular verbs**. This means that they form the past tense merely by adding **-ed, -d,** or **-t** to the main verb: *race, raced.* This simple procedure makes regular verbs easy to identify. Some verbs, however, do not form their past tense in this regular way. For this reason, they are called **irregular verbs**. Most irregular verbs form the past tense by having a **vowel spelling change** in the word. For example: *sing, sang, sung* or *eat, ate, eaten.*

To decide if a verb is regular or irregular, remember these two things:

1. Look only at the main verb. If the main verb is made past tense with an *-ed, -d, or -t* ending, it is a regular verb. (race, raced, raced)
2. Look only at the main verb. If the main verb is made past tense with a vowel spelling change, it is an irregular verb. (sing, sang, sung)

A partial listing of the most common irregular verbs is on the irregular verb chart located in Reference 23 on page 17 in the student book. Refer to this chart whenever necessary.

Example: Identify each verb as regular or irregular and put **R** or **I** in the blank. Then, write the past tense form.

eat	I	ate		pay	R	paid		tempt	R	tempted
jump	R	jumped		forget	I	forgot		swim	I	swam

Reference 52: Story Elements Outline

1. **Main Idea (Tell the problem or situation that needs a solution.)**
   Jared knew his mom was not feeling well and wanted to do something nice for her.
2. **Setting (Tell when and where the story takes place, either clearly stated or implied.)**
   When - The story takes place when Jared's mother could use some help. Where – The story takes place at Jared's home.
3. **Character (Tell whom or what the story is about.)**
   The two characters are Jared and his mother.
4. **Plot (Tell what the characters in the story do and what happens to them.)**
   The story is about a young man who sets out to surprise his mother and whose thoughtfulness overwhelms her.
5. **Ending (Use a strong ending that will bring the story to a close.)**
   The story ends with the mother's being overcome with emotion.

Jared's Surprise

Jared didn't very often get the urge to do household chores. But, yesterday, he thought he'd do something nice for his mom because she hadn't been feeling well lately.

"Mom, you just rest," he said. "I'm going to surprise you." With that, he turned and walked down the long hall toward the laundry room. "Whites," he said to himself thoughtfully. "Whites only in this load!" He had to keep reminding himself of the things he had heard his mother say as she did the laundry.

When his mom heard the washer running, she got up from her bed to see what was happening. As she turned the corner into the laundry room, she stopped dead in her tracks. "Jared, what are you doing?"

"Surprise!" he replied happily, grinning from ear to ear. "Just one thing less you'll need to worry about when you start feeling better. I did all our laundry!" Jared beamed as he gave his mother a hug.

"Jared, I can't tell you how much I appreciate your thoughtfulness," said Jared's mom as she looked at the piles of clothes scattered all over the laundry room. With one last look at the pink sheets, Jared's mom gave her son another hug as she made her way back to bed.

Reference 54: Simple Verb Tenses

When you are writing paragraphs, you must use verbs that are in the same tense. Tense means time. The tense of a verb shows the time of the action. There are three basic tenses that show when an action takes place. They are **present tense, past tense,** and **future tense**. These tenses are known as the simple tenses.

1. The **simple present tense** shows that something is happening now, in the present. The present tense form usually has *-s, -es, or plain ending*.
   (Regular present tense form: cheer, cheers) (Irregular present tense form: fall, falls)
   (**Examples:** The fans <u>cheer</u> for their team. The rain <u>falls</u> slowly.)

2. The **simple past tense** shows that something has happened sometime in the past. The regular past tense form ends in *-ed, -d, or -t.* Most irregular past tense forms should be memorized.
   (Regular past tense form: cheered) (Irregular past tense form: fell)
   (**Examples:** The fans <u>cheered</u> for their team. The rain <u>fell</u> slowly.)

3. The **future tense** shows that something will happen sometime in the future. The future tense form always has the helping verb *will* or *shall* before the main verb.
   (Regular future tense form: will cheer) (Irregular future tense form: will fall)
   (**Examples:** The fans <u>will cheer</u> for their team. The rain <u>will fall</u> slowly.)

Simple Present Tense	Simple Past Tense	Simple Future Tense
What to look for: **one verb** with -s, -es, or plain ending.	What to look for: **one verb** with -ed, -d, -t, or irr spelling change.	What to look for: **will** or **shall** with a main verb.
1. He <u>stands</u> on his head.	3. He <u>stood</u> on his head.	5. He <u>will stand</u> on his head.
2. She <u>plays</u> the harmonica.	4. She <u>played</u> the harmonica.	6. She <u>will play</u> the harmonica.

Reference 55: Tenses of Helping Verbs

1. If there is only a main verb in a sentence, the tense is determined by the main verb and will be either present tense or past tense.
2. If there is a helping verb with a main verb, the tense of both verbs will be determined by the helping verb, not the main verb.

<u>Since the helping verb determines the tense</u>, it is important to learn the tenses of the 14 helping verbs you will be using. You should memorize the list below so you will never have trouble with tenses.

> **Present tense helping verbs: am, is, are, has, have, do, does**
> **Past tense helping verbs: was, were, had, did, been**
> **Future tense helping verbs: will, shall**

If you use one of the present tense helping verbs, you are considered in present tense even though the main verb has an -*ed* ending and even though it doesn't sound like present tense. (*I have walked - present tense.*) In later grades, you will learn that certain helping verbs help form other tenses called the perfect tenses.

Example 1: Underline each verb or verb phrase. Identify the verb tense by writing a number **1** for present tense, a number **2** for past tense, or a number **3** for future tense. Write the past tense form and **R** or **I** for Regular or Irregular.

Verb Tense		Main Verb Past Tense Form	R or I
1	1. The boy <u>rides</u> his bicycle.	rode	I
2	2. The engineer <u>had</u> <u>consulted</u> the mayor.	consulted	R
3	3. Tomorrow, I <u>will</u> <u>stain</u> the deck.	stained	R

Example 2: List the present tense and past tense helping verbs below.

Present tense:	1. **am**	2. **is**	3. **are**	4. **has**	5. **have**	6. **do**	7. **does**
Past tense:	8. **was**	9. **were**	10. **had**	11. **did**	12. **been**		

Reference 56: Principal Parts of Verbs

Every main verb has four principal forms, or parts. All the forms of a main verb are made by using one of the four principal parts. The four principal parts of main verbs are called **present, present participle, past,** and **past participle**. The principal parts are the same for regular and irregular verbs.

1. **Present principal part** - has a present tense main verb and no helping verb.
   (He <u>walks</u> home. They <u>walk</u> home.) (He <u>grows</u> fast. They <u>grow</u> fast.)

2. **Past principal part** - has a past tense main verb and no helping verb.
   (He <u>walked</u> home.) (He <u>grew</u> fast.)

3. **Past participle principal part** - has past tense main verb and present or past tense helping verb.
   (He <u>has</u> <u>walked</u> home.) (He <u>has</u> <u>grown</u> fast.)

4. **Present participle principal part** - has a main verb ending in -*ing* and a present or past tense helping verb. (He <u>is</u> <u>walking</u> home.) (He <u>is</u> <u>growing</u> fast.)

Examples: Principal parts of the regular verb *walk*: walk(s), walked, has walked, is walking
Examples: Principal parts of the irregular verb *grow*: grow(s), grew, has grown, is growing

Remember, you must not confuse the past principal part of the verb with the past participle principal part. The past principal part never has a helping verb. The past participle principal part always has a helping verb.

Reference 57: Changing Tenses in Paragraphs

Guided Example 1: Change the underlined present tense verbs in Paragraph 1 to past tense verbs in Paragraph 2.

Paragraph 1: Present Tense

On weekends, Sarah **makes** pancakes for her family's breakfast. As soon as she **hears** footsteps in the distance, she **starts** mixing the batter and **begins** heating the griddle. Once the procession of husband and daughters **arrives** at the kitchen door, she **pours** batter the size of quarters on the hot griddle. As the flapjacks **sizzle** in hot oil, Sarah **urges** everyone to take a seat. The feast **is** about to begin.

Paragraph 2: Past Tense

On weekends, Sarah **made** pancakes for her family's breakfast. As soon as she **heard** footsteps in the distance, she **started** mixing the batter and **began** heating the griddle. Once the procession of husband and daughters **arrived** at the kitchen door, she **poured** batter the size of quarters on the hot griddle. As the flapjacks **sizzled** in hot oil, Sarah **urged** everyone to take a seat. The feast **was** about to begin.

Guided Example 2: Change the underlined mixed tense verbs in Paragraph 1 to past tense verbs in Paragraph 2.

Paragraph 3: Mixed Tenses

The excited couple **is planning** a trip to the beach for their anniversary. They eagerly **contacted** a local travel agent. The agent **suggests** renting a condo for a week on the Mississippi shoreline. Their two children **look** at pictures of beaches in travel magazines. The family carefully **saves** every extra penny for their vacation. Finally, the big day **arrives**, but no one **was going**. They all **have** chicken pox!

Paragraph 4: Past Tense

The excited couple **was planning** a trip to the beach for their anniversary. They eagerly **contacted** a local travel agent. The agent **suggested** renting a condo for a week on the Mississippi shoreline. Their two children **looked** at pictures of beaches in travel magazines. The family carefully **saved** every extra penny for their vacation. Finally, the big day **arrived**, but no one **was going**. They all **had** chicken pox!

Reference 58: This reference is on page 43.

Reference 59: Contraction Chart			Pronoun	Contraction

AM
I am – I'm

IS
is not – isn't
he is – he's
she is – she's
it is – it's
who is – who's
that is – that's
what is – what's
there is – there's

ARE
are not – aren't
you are – you're
we are – we're
they are – they're

WAS, WERE
was not – wasn't
were not – weren't

DO, DOES, DID
do not – don't
does not – doesn't
did not – didn't

CAN
cannot – can't

LET
let us – let's

HAS
has not – hasn't
he has – he's
she has – she's

HAVE
have not – haven't
I have – I've
you have – you've
we have – we've
they have – they've

HAD
had not – hadn't
I had – I'd
he had – he'd
she had – she'd
you had – you'd
we had – we'd
they had – they'd

WILL / SHALL
will not – won't
I will – I'll
he will – he'll
she will – she'll
you will – you'll
we will – we'll
they will – they'll

WOULD
would not – wouldn't
I would – I'd
he would – he'd
she would – she'd
you would – you'd
we would – we'd
they would – they'd

SHOULD, COULD
should not – shouldn't
could not – couldn't

Pronoun / Contraction

its
(owns)
its coat

it's
(it is)
it's cute

your
(owns)
your car

you're
(you are)
you're right

their
(owns)
their house

they're
(they are)
they're gone

whose
(owns)
whose cat

who's
(who is)
who's going

Reference 60: Degrees of Adjectives

The **Simple Form** is used when no comparison is made. There are no rules for the simple form. (**fast, nervous**)

The **Comparative Form** is used to compare **TWO** people, places, or things.

The **Superlative Form** is used to compare **THREE** or more people, places, or things.

Rule 1. Use **-er** with most 1 or 2 syllable words. (**faster**) Use **more** with **-ful** words or whenever the **-er** sounds awkward. (**more nervous**) Use **more** for all 3-or-more syllable words.

Rule 2. Use **-est** with most 1 or 2 syllable words. (**fastest**) Use **most** with **-ful** words or whenever the **-est** sounds awkward. (**most nervous**) Use **most** for all 3-or-more syllable words.

Irregular Adjectives Have No Rule Numbers and Have to be Memorized

Simple Adjective		Comparative		Superlative	
1. good	3. little (amount)	5. better	7. less or lesser	9. best	11. least
2. bad, ill	4. much, many	6. worse	8. more	10. worst	12. most

Sentence Examples

1. Daniel bought a good hat. 2. Daniel bought a better hat than Scott. 3. Daniel bought the best hat of all the other students.

Practice: Write the rule numbers and the different forms for the adjectives below. For irregular forms, write **Irr** in the box.

Simple Adjective Form	Rule Box	Comparative Adjective Form	Rule Box	Superlative Adjective Form
1. agreeable	1	more agreeable	2	most agreeable
2. lucky	1	luckier	2	luckiest
3. ill	Irr	worse	Irr	worst

4. I am **taller** than Sam. (tall) 5. Of all the girls, she was the **most eager** to go. (eager) 6. She reads **better** than Sue. (good)

Reference 61: Double Negatives

Negative Words That Begin With **N**					Other Negative Words	Negative Prefixes
neither	no	no one	not (n't)	nowhere	barely, hardly, scarcely	dis, non, un
never	nobody	none	nothing			

Three Ways to Correct a Double Negative

Rule 1: **Change** the second negative to a positive:
Wrong: Walter **couldn't** eat **nothing**. Right: Walter **couldn't** eat **anything**.

Rule 2: **Take out** the negative part of a contraction:
Wrong: Samantha **shouldn't** ask **nothing**. Right: Samantha **should** ask **nothing**.

Rule 3: **Remove** the first negative word (possibility of a verb change):
Wrong: Warren **didn't** want **nothing**. Right: Warren **wanted nothing**.

Changing Negative Words to Positive Words

1. Change *no* or *none* to *any*.
2. Change *nobody* to *anybody*.
3. Change *no one* to *anyone*.
4. Change *nothing* to *anything*.
5. Change *nowhere* to *anywhere*.
6. Change *never* to *ever*.
7. Change *neither* to *either*.
8. Remove the *n't* from a contraction.

Examples: Underline the negative words in each sentence. Rewrite each sentence and correct the double negative mistake as indicated by the rule number in parentheses at the end of the sentence.

1. Sarah doesn't have no money for the fair. (Rule 3) **Sarah has no money for the fair.**
2. He can't hardly wait for our science contest. (Rule 2) **He can hardly wait for our science contest.**
3. She hasn't done nothing for the fundraiser. (Rule 1) **She hasn't done anything for the fundraiser.**

Reference 62: Guidelines for Descriptive Writing

1. **When describing people,** it is helpful to notice these types of details: appearance, walk, voice, manner, gestures, personality traits, any special incident related to the person being described, and any striking details that will help make that person stand out in your mind.

2. **When describing places or things,** it is helpful to notice these types of details: the physical features of a place or thing (color, texture, smell, shape, size, age), any unusual features, any special incident related to the place or thing being described, and whether or not the place or thing is special to you.

3. **When describing nature,** it is helpful to notice these types of details: the special features of the season, the sights, smells, sounds, colors, animals, insects, birds, and any special incident related to the scene being described.

4. **When describing an incident or an event,** it is helpful to notice these types of details: the order in which the event takes place, any specific facts that will keep the story moving from a beginning to an ending, the answers to any of the *who, what, when, where, why,* and *how* questions that the reader needs to know, and especially the details that will create a clear picture, such as how things look, sound, smell, feel, etc.

Reference 63: Descriptive Paragraph Guidelines

A. Sentence 1 is the topic sentence that introduces **what is being described**.
B. For sentences 2-8, use **the descriptive details** in Reference 62.
C. Sentence 6 is a concluding sentence that **restates or relates back to the topic sentence**.

A Picnic at the Park

Every Fourth of July, my aunt and uncle pack a picnic basket and have lunch at one of the wildlife parks. Despite the pesky ants, they enjoy grilling hamburgers and hot dogs over an open fire. And while they are enjoying their sandwiches, they can watch and listen to a variety of birds in flight. Occasionally, an almost-tame deer wanders out of nearby woods and adds magic to their outing. They find that eating out in the open and breathing in the fresh air is invigorating. It is hard to imagine that my aunt and uncle would ever surrender this ritual.

Reference 64: Personal Pronoun-Antecedent Agreement

     antecedent   *pronoun*   *antecedent*   *pronoun*   *pronoun*

1. The *nanny* fell and broke *her* foot.   2. The *nanny* fell. *She* somehow broke *her* foot.

1. Decide if the antecedent is singular or plural, and then choose the pronoun that agrees in number.

   If the antecedent is singular, the pronoun must be singular. (man - he, him, his, etc.)
   If the antecedent is plural, the pronoun must be plural. (men - they, them, their, etc.)

2. Decide if the antecedent is male or female, and then choose the pronoun that agrees in gender.

   If the antecedent is masculine, the pronoun must be masculine gender. (boy-he)
   If the antecedent is feminine, the pronoun must be feminine gender. (girl-she)
   If the antecedent is neither masculine nor feminine, the pronoun must be neuter gender. (book-it)

   (The plural pronouns *they* and *them* also show neuter gender. The **trees** are dead. **They** burned in the fire.)

Guided Practice for Pronoun-Antecedent Agreement

Choose an answer from the pronoun choices in parentheses. Then, fill in the rest of the columns according to the titles. (**S** or **P** stands for singular or plural.)

Pronoun-Antecedent Agreement	Pronoun choice	S or P	Antecedent	S or P
1. The snake arched (<u>its</u>, their) back in self-defense.	its	S	snake	S
2. The actress stared at (<u>her</u>, their) audience lovingly.	her	S	actress	S
3. Her uncles need (his, <u>their</u>) black shoes.	their	P	uncles	P

Reference 58: Predicate Noun and Linking Verb

1. A **predicate noun** is a noun or pronoun after the verb that means the same thing as the subject.

2. A **predicate noun** is labeled as *PrN*. (Label a **predicate pronoun** as **PrP**.)

3. To find the **predicate noun**, ask WHAT? or WHO? after the verb.

4. A **predicate noun** is often called a predicate nominative.

5. A **predicate noun** always comes after a linking verb.

6. A **linking verb** links, or connects, the subject to a predicate noun or a predicate pronoun.

Sample Sentence for the exact words to say to find the linking verb and predicate noun.

1. Sue is an excellent swimmer.
2. Who is an excellent swimmer? Sue - SN
3. What is being said about Sue? Sue is - V
4. Sue is who? swimmer - verify the noun
5. Does swimmer mean the same thing as Sue? Yes.
6. Swimmer - *PrN* (Say: swimmer - predicate noun.)
7. Is - LV (Say: Is - linking verb.)
8. What kind of swimmer? excellent - Adj
9. An - A

10. SN LV PrN P4 Check
    (Say: Subject Noun, Linking Verb, Predicate Noun, Pattern 4, Check.)
    (This first check is to make sure the "L" is added to the verb.)
11. Linking verb - check again.
    ("Check again" means to check for prepositional phrases and then go through the rest of the Question and Answer Flow.)
12. No prepositional phrases.
13. Period, statement, declarative sentence
14. Go back to the verb - divide the complete subject from the complete predicate.
15. Is there an adverb exception? No.
16. Is this sentence in a natural or inverted order? Natural - no change.

Reference 65: The Difference Between Action Verbs and Linking Verbs

An action verb shows action. It tells what the subject does. A linking verb does not show action. It does not tell what the subject does. A linking verb is called a state of being verb because it tells **what the subject is or is like**. To decide if a verb is linking or action, remember these two things:

1. A linking verb may have a noun in the predicate that means the same thing as the subject:

To show what the subject **is** means the linking verb connects the subject to a noun in the predicate that means the same thing as the subject. This noun is called a predicate noun and is identified with the abbreviation **PrN**.

    SN LV   PrN   SP LV   PrN   SN LV   PrN   SN LV   PrN
<u>Arnold</u> **was** a (gymnast).   <u>She</u> **is** a (teacher).   The <u>tour</u> **is** an (education).   His <u>car</u> **was** a (jalopy).

2. A linking verb may also have an adjective in the predicate that tells what kind of subject it is:

To show what the subject **is like** means the linking verb connects the subject to an adjective in the predicate that tells <u>what kind</u> of subject it is. This adjective is called a predicate adjective and is identified with the abbreviation **PA**. *(What kind of dog? hungry – PA) (What kind of boat? expensive – PA) (What kind of cheese? moldy – PA)*

     SN LV PA   SN LV   PA   SN   LV PA   SN   LV   PA
That <u>dog</u> **is** (hungry).   The <u>boat</u> **was** (expensive).   The <u>cheese</u> **is** (moldy).   The <u>roads</u> **are** (crooked).

These are the most common linking verbs: *am, is, are, was, were, be, been, seem, become.*

These sensory verbs can be linking or action: *taste, sound, smell, feel, look.*

Good rule to follow: If a sentence has a predicate noun (**PrN**) or a predicate adjective (**PA**), it has a linking verb. If a sentence <u>does not have</u> a predicate noun (**PrN**) or a predicate adjective (**PA**), it has an action verb.

Example: Underline each subject and fill in each column according to the title.

	List each Verb	Write PrN, PA, or None	Write L or A
1. The <u>groceries</u> are heavy.	are	PA	L
2. An <u>apricot</u> is a fruit.	is	PrN	L
3. The <u>gnat</u> buzzed in my ear.	buzzed	None	A

Reference 66: Rules for the Plurals of Nouns with Different Endings

1. "ch, sh, z, s, ss, x," add "es."
2. a vowel plus "y," add an "s."
3. a consonant plus "y," change "y" to "i" and add "es."
4. "f" or "fe," change the "f" or "fe" to "v" and add "es."
5. irregular nouns-change spellings completely.
6. "f" or "ff," add "s."
7. a vowel plus "o," add "s."
8. a consonant plus "o," add "es."
9. stays the same for S and P.
10. regular nouns, add "s."

Use the rules above to write the correct plural form of these nouns:

	Rule	Plural Form			Rule	Plural Form
1. obey	**2**	**obeys**	2. half		**4**	**halves**
3. hoof	**6 or 4**	**hoofs or hooves**	4. fish		**9 or 1**	**fish or fishes**

Reference 67: The Five Parts of a Friendly Letter

1. Heading
1. Box or street address of writer
2. City, state, zip code of writer
3. Date letter was written
4. Placement: upper right-hand corner

2. Friendly Greeting or Salutation
1. Begins with *Dear*
2. Names person receiving the letter
3. Has comma after person's name
4. Placement: at left margin, two lines below heading

3. Body
1. Tells reason the letter was written
2. Can have one or more paragraphs
3. Has indented paragraphs
4. Is placed one line after the greeting
5. Skips one line between each paragraph

4. Closing
1. Closes letter with a personal phrase-(Your friend, With love,)
2. Capitalizes only first word
3. Is followed by a comma
4. Is placed two lines below the body
5. Begins just to the right of the middle of the letter

5. Signature
1. Tells who wrote the letter
2. Is usually signed in cursive
3. Uses first name only unless there is a question as to which friend or relative you are
4. Is placed beneath the closing

Friendly Letter Example

1. Heading
P.O. Box 372
Akron, IN 18043
August 19, 20___

2. Friendly Greeting, (or Salutation)
Dear Mary Jo,

3. Body (Indent Paragraphs)

How wonderful that you are coming to spend the holidays with us. I can hardly wait. Mom plans to make your favorite dessert while you are here.

4. Closing,
Your cousin,

5. Signature
Lydia

Reference 68: Envelope Parts	Friendly Envelope Example

The return address:
1. Name of the person writing the letter
2. Box or street address of the writer
3. City, state, zip code of the writer

The mailing address:
1. Name of the person receiving the letter
2. Street address of the person receiving the letter
3. City, state, zip code of the person receiving the letter

Return Address
Lydia Martin
468 Pickwick Road
Stanton, IA 92434

Stamp

Mailing Address
Mary Jo Faulkner
P.O. Box 372
Akron, IN 18043

Reference 69: Four Types of Business Letters

Four common reasons to write business letters and information about the four types:

1. If you need to send for information - letter of inquiry.
2. If you want to order a product - letter of request or order.
3. If you want to express an opinion - letter to an editor or official.
4. If you want to complain about a product - letter of complaint.

Letter of Inquiry	Letter of Request or Order
1. Ask for information or answers to your questions. 2. Keep the letter short and to the point. 3. Word the letter so that there can be no question as to what it is you need to know.	1. Carefully and clearly describe the product. 2. Keep the letter short and to the point. 3. Include information on how and where the product should be shipped. 4. Include information on how you will pay for the product.

Letter to an Editor or Official	Letter of Complaint About a Product
1. Clearly explain the problem or situation. 2. Offer your opinion of the cause and possible solutions. 3. Support your opinions with facts and examples. 4. Suggest ways to change or improve the situation.	1. Carefully and clearly describe the product. 2. Describe the problem and what may have caused it. (Don't spend too much time explaining how unhappy you are.) 3. Explain any action you have already taken to solve the problem. 4. End your letter with the action you would like the company to take to solve the problem.

Reference 70: Business Letter Example

1. HEADING

615 Calumet Drive
Arlington, VT 49122
March 16, 20___

2. INSIDE ADDRESS

Dr. Forrest Garner
Garner Dental Clinic
363 Fulton Manor
Brighton, TN 82821

3. FORMAL GREETING, (OR SALUTATION)

Dear Dr. Garner:

4. BODY (INDENT PARAGRAPHS)

   My uncle broke his lower denture in half while eating popcorn last night. If you will send me a tube of your famous adhesive, I will gladly send you a money order to pay for it.

5. FORMAL CLOSING,

Most sincerely,

6. SIGNATURE

Fulton Asher

Reference 71: Envelope Parts	Business Envelope Example
The return address: 1. Name of the person writing the letter 2. Box or street address of the writer 3. City, state, zip code of the writer **The mailing address:** 1. Name of the person receiving the letter 2. Name of the company receiving the letter 3. Street address of the person receiving the letter 4. City, state, zip code of the person receiving the letter	**Return Address** Stamp Fulton Asher 615 Calumet Drive Arlington, VT 49122 **Mailing Address** Dr. Forrest Garner Garner Dental Clinic 363 Fulton Manor Brighton, TN 82821

Reference 72: Thank-You Notes		
For a Gift		**For an Action**
What - Thank you for... (tell color, kind, and item) **Use -** Tell how the gift is used. **Thanks -** I appreciate your remembering me with this special gift.		**What -** Thank you for... (tell action) **Helped -** Tell how the action helped **Thanks -** I appreciate your thinking of me at this time.

Example 1: Gift

4142 Dogwood Trail
Austin, NV 21676
June 27, 20__

Dear Lois,

   How could I ever thank you enough for the autographed copy of Jesse Stuart's book? It is a treasure, and I will add it to my collection of rare books.

Most sincerely,

Wanda

Example 2: Action

46401 Bursley Road
Grafton, OH 65703
July 21, 20__

Dear Brandon,

   Thanks for helping me change the flat tire on Dad's truck last night. I doubt that I could have done it without your help. You are a true friend!

Appreciatively,

Lance

Reference 73: Invitations

1.	What	– a surprise birthday party
2.	Who	– for Hunter Davis
3.	Where	– at Barton Community Center
4.	When	– on Saturday, August 7, at 7:00 p.m.
5.	Whipped Cream	– hope you can join us!

238 Virginia Cove
Upton, Florida 44602
July 30, 20__

Dear Lonnie,

    We are having a <u>surprise birthday party</u> for <u>Hunter Davis</u> on <u>Saturday evening, August 7, at 7:00</u> and <u>hope</u> that <u>you can join us</u>. It will be held at <u>Barton Community Center</u> on Merrill Drive. There will be all kinds of good things to eat. Be there!

Your friends,
Jerry and Jared Wagner

Reference 74: Parts of a Book

THE FRONT:

1. **Title Page.** This page has the full title of the book, the author's name, the illustrator's name, the name of the publishing company, and the city where the book was published.

2. **Copyright Page.** This page is right after the title page and tells the year in which the book was published and who owns the copyright. If the book has an ISBN number (International Standard Book Number), it is listed here.

3. **Preface** (also called **introduction**). If a book has this page, it will come before the table of contents and will usually tell you briefly why the book was written and what it is about.

4. **Table of Contents.** This section lists the major divisions of the book by units or chapters and tells their page numbers.

5. **Body.** This is the main section, or text, of the book.

THE BACK:

6. **Appendix.** This section includes extra informative material such as maps, charts, tables, diagrams, letters, etc. It is always wise to find out what is in the appendix, since it may contain supplementary material that you could otherwise find only by going to the library.

7. **Glossary.** This section is like a dictionary and gives the meanings of some of the important words in the book.

8. **Bibliography.** This section includes a list of books used by the author. It could serve as a guide for further reading on a topic.

9. **Index.** This will probably be your most useful section. The purpose of the index is to help you quickly locate information about the topics in the book. It has an alphabetical list of specific topics and tells on which page that information can be found. It is similar to the table of contents, but it is much more detailed.

Reference 75: Card Catalog Cards		
Author Card	**Title Card**	**Subject Card**

812.83
Author-Jensen, R. K.
Title   <u>Looking for Limericks</u>
    Ill. by Meg Brady
    Sumpter Press, Albany
    (c1999) 182p.
	812.83
	Title <u>Looking for Limericks</u>
	Author-Jensen, R. K.
	    Ill. by Meg Brady
	    Sumpter Press, Albany
	    (c1999) 182p.
		812.83
		Topic Types of Poems
		Author-Jensen, R. K.
		Title <u>Looking for Limericks</u>
		    Ill. by Meg Brady
		    Sumpter Press, Albany
		    (c1999) 182p.

Reference 76: Sample Index		

L
Layovers, 36–39, 102
	S
	Sleep,
	    at rest areas, 104–107, 109; daytime, 40–41;
	    nighttime, 42–43; at truck stops, 111–115
		T
		Time off, 57
		Travel schedules, 86

Reference 77: Sample Table of Contents

CONTENTS

CHAPTER	TITLE	PAGE
1	*What It Takes to be a Trucker*....................................	1
2	*Life on the Road*..	24
3	*A Few Days Off the Road*	46
4	*Scheduling Long-Distance Trips*	58
5	*Daily Recovery: Where to Stop*	90

Reference 78A: Outline Information

<u>Outline Guide</u>

Title

I. Introduction

II. Main Topic (First main point)
  A. Subtopic (Supports first main point)
    1. Details (Supports subtopic)
    2. Details (Supports subtopic)
  B. Subtopic (Supports first main point)
  C. Subtopic (Supports first main point)

III. Main Topic (Second main point)
  A. Subtopic (Supports second main point)
  B. Subtopic (Supports second main point)

IV. Main Topic (Third main point)
  A. Subtopic (Supports third main point)
  B. Subtopic (Supports third main point)

V. Conclusion

<u>Sample Outline</u>

Seasonal Tasks Outdoors

I. Introduction

II. Spring tasks
  A. Rake fallen leaves
    1. Mulch shrubs
    2. Create compost pile
  B. Weed yard
  C. Plant garden

III. Summer tasks
  A. Tend garden crops
  B. Mow grass

IV. Autumn tasks
  A. Harvest produce
  B. Plant spring bulbs

V. Conclusion

Reference 78B: Outline Information

First, an outline has a TITLE.

- At first, your outline title should be the same or similar to your narrowed topic. This will help you stay focused on the main idea of your report. If you decide to change the title for your final paper, you must remember to change your outline title.

- Capitalizing rules for titles are the same for outlines as for final papers: Capitalize the first word, the last word, and all the important words in between them. Conjunctions, articles, and prepositions with fewer than five letters are not usually capitalized unless they are the first or last word. Titles for reports are not underlined or placed in quotation marks unless the title is a quotation.

Second, an outline has Roman numerals denoting MAIN TOPICS.

- There must always be two or more Roman numerals. There can never be just one. For each Roman numeral, there is a paragraph. (Three Roman numerals - three paragraphs.)

- The information following a Roman numeral is called the main topic and gives the main idea, or main point, of each paragraph. It will be used to form the topic sentence of the paragraph.

- Every first word in a main topic is always capitalized.

- The periods after the Roman numerals must be lined up under each other.

Third, an outline has capital letters denoting SUBTOPICS.

- There must always be two or more capital letters. If you only have one, do not put it in the outline. Each capital letter is indented under the first word of the main topic.

- The information beside a capital letter is called the subtopic and gives details that support the main topic, or main point of the paragraph.

- Every first word in a subtopic is always capitalized.

- The periods after the capital letters must be lined up under each other.

Fourth, an outline sometimes has Arabic numerals denoting DETAILS.

- There must always be two or more Arabic numerals. If you only have one, do not put it on the outline. Each Arabic numeral is indented under the first word of the subtopic.

- The information beside an Arabic numeral is called a detail and tells specific information about the subtopic of the paragraph.

- Every first word in a detail is always capitalized.

- The periods after the Arabic numerals must be lined up under each other.

Reference 79: Parallel Form for Outlines

Parallel Form

1. All the main topics in an outline should be in parallel form. This means that all the main topics should begin in the same way: all nouns, all verbs, all noun phrases, all verb phrases, all prepositional phrases, etc. If necessary, change or rearrange the words of your outline so they are parallel.

   (**I. Spring tasks II. Summer tasks III. Autumn tasks**) or (**I. A farmer's spring tasks II. A farmer's summer tasks III. A farmer's autumn tasks**)

2. All the subtopics under Roman numeral II must be in the same form. The subtopics under Roman numeral III must be in the same form, but Roman numeral II subtopics do not have to be in the same form as Roman numeral III subtopics, etc.

   (A. **Rake** fallen leaves B. **Weed** yard C. **Plant** garden)   (A. **Tend** garden crops B. **Mow** grass)

3. All the details under Subtopic A must be in the same form. The details under Subtopic B must be in the same form, but Subtopic A details do not have to be in the same form as Subtopic B details.

   (1. **Mulch** shrubs 2. **Create** compost pile)

Notes

PRACTICE

SECTION

Chapter 1, Lesson 5, Practice

Exercise 1: Identify each pair of words as synonyms or antonyms by putting parentheses ( ) around **syn** or **ant**. For number 5, write two synonym words and identify them with **syn**. For number 6, write two antonym words and identify them with **ant**.

1. prodigy, genius	syn	ant	3. construction, dilapidation	syn	ant	5.
2. timid, audacious	syn	ant	4. destroy, abolish	syn	ant	6.

Chapter 2, Lesson 3, Practice 1

Put the end mark and the abbreviation for each kind of sentence in the blanks below.

1. Check your homework carefully _____

2. Did you clean your room _____

3. The firemen are on their way _____

4. I have already packed my suitcase for our trip _____

Chapter 2, Lesson 3, Practice 2

On notebook paper, write a sentence to demonstrate each of these four kinds of sentences:
(1) Declarative (2) Interrogative (3) Exclamatory (4) Imperative. Write the correct punctuation and the abbreviation that identifies it at the end. Use these abbreviations: **D**, **Int**, **E**, **Imp**.

Chapter 2, Lesson 3, Practice 3

Match the definitions. Write the correct letter beside each numbered concept.

_____ 1. exclamatory sentence

_____ 2. a/an are also called

_____ 3. adjective modifies

_____ 4. verb question

_____ 5. a definite article

_____ 6. subject-noun question (thing)

_____ 7. article adjective can be called

_____ 8. makes a request or gives a command

_____ 9. noun

_____ 10. subject-noun question (person)

_____ 11. punctuation for declarative

_____ 12. adverb modifies

A.   verb, adjective, or adverb

B.   who

C.   what is being said about

D.   person, place, thing

E.   what

F.   period

G.   shows strong feeling

H.   indefinite articles

I.   noun or pronoun

J.   the

K.   noun marker

L.   imperative sentence

Chapter 2, Lesson 3, Practice 4

Fill in the blank: Write the answer for each question.

1. What are the three article adjectives? _____

2. What word tells what the subject does? _____

Chapter 3, Lesson 1, Practice

Directions: Look at the classified sentence below and underline the complete subject once and the complete predicate twice. Then, complete the table below.

```
          A      Adj      SN        V     Adv   Adv
  SN  V    An enormous elephant / stomped angrily around!  E
  P1
```

List the Noun Used	List the Noun Job	Singular or Plural	Common or Proper	Simple Subject	Simple Predicate

---

Chapter 3, Lesson 2, Practice

Directions: Classify the sentence below. Underline the complete subject once and the complete predicate twice. Then, complete the table.

The   beautiful   wild   horses   raced   swiftly   away.

List the Noun Used	List the Noun Job	Singular or Plural	Common or Proper	Simple Subject	Simple Predicate
horses	subject raced	plural	common	horses	raced

Finding One Part of Speech: For each sentence, write **SN** above the simple subject and **V** above the simple predicate. Underline the word(s) for the part of speech listed to the left of each sentence.

Adjective(s): 1. The crisp, brown leaves wave loudly every autumn.

Adverb(s): 2. The flustered young man finally walked very quickly away.

Noun(s): 3. Several frightened green frogs leaped hurriedly away.

Adjective(s): 4. The dog slowly limped away.

Verb(s): 5. The actors performed extremely well.

Chapter 3, Lesson 3, Practice

Put this 3-part assignment on notebook paper: (1) Write the four parts of speech that you have studied so far (in any order). (2) Write out the Question and Answer Flow in exact order for the Practice Sentence below. (3) Classify the sentence.

Practice Sentence: The large frightened crowd dispersed quickly.

Chapter 3, Lesson 5, Practice Writing Page

Use the three-point outline form below to guide you as you write a three-point expository paragraph.

Write a topic: _____

Write 3 points to list about the topic.

1. _____ 2. _____ 3. _____

Sentence #1   Topic sentence (*Use words in the topic and tell how many points will be used.*)

_____

Sentence #2   3-point sentence (*List your 3 points in the order that you will present them.*)

_____

Sentence #3   State your first point in a complete sentence.

_____

Sentence #4   Write a supporting sentence for the first point.

_____

Sentence #5   State your second point in a complete sentence.

_____

Sentence #6   Write a supporting sentence for the second point.

_____

Sentence #7   State your third point in a complete sentence.

_____

Sentence #8   Write a supporting sentence for the third point.

_____

Sentence #9   Concluding sentence (*Restate the topic sentence and add an extra thought.*)

_____

Student Note: Rewrite your nine-sentence paragraph on a sheet of notebook paper. Be sure to indent and use the checklists to help you edit your paragraph. Make sure you re-read your paragraph several times slowly.

Chapter 4, Lesson 3, Practice 1

Rule 1: A singular subject must use a singular verb form that ends in **s**: *is, was, has, does,* or *verbs ending with* **s** or **es**.

Rule 2: A plural subject, a compound subject, or the subject **YOU** must use a plural verb form that has **no s** ending: *are, were, do, have,* or *verbs without* **s** or **es** *endings.* (A plural verb form is also called the *plain form.*)

Examples: For each sentence, do these four things: 1. Write the subject. 2. Write **S** if the subject is singular or **P** if the subject is plural. 3. Write the rule number. 4. Underline the correct verb in the sentence.

Subject	S or P	Rule	
			1. The eagles (was, were) flying upside down.
			2. Tom and his sister (is, are) good sports.
			3. My aunt (was, were) fearful of the plane ride.

Chapter 4, Lesson 3, Practice 2

On notebook paper, write a Practice and Improved Sentence, using these labels:

A Adj Adj SN V Adv Adv

Chapter 4, Lesson 3, Practice 3

Put this 3-part assignment on notebook paper: (1) Write the four parts of speech that you have studied so far (in any order). (2) Write out the Question and Answer Flow in exact order for the sentence listed. (3) Classify the sentence.

Practice Sentence: Unintentionally, the young mother spoke quite harshly.

Chapter 5, Lesson 3, Practice 1

Write the five parts of speech that you have studied so far (in any order) on notebook paper.

Chapter 5, Lesson 3, Practice 2

Choose one set of labels below and write a Practice and Improved Sentence on notebook paper.

A Adv Adj SN V Adv P A Adj OP or **A Adj Adj SN P A OP V Adv P A Adj OP**

Chapter 6, Lesson 1, Practice 1

Write the five parts of speech that you have studied so far (in any order) on notebook paper.

Chapter 6, Lesson 1, Practice 2

Choose one set of labels below and write a Practice and Improved Sentence on notebook paper.

A Adv Adj SN V Adv P A Adj OP P A OP or **A Adj SN P A OP V P A Adj OP P A OP**

Chapter 10, Lesson 3, Practice

Use the Editing Guide below each sentence to know how many capitalization and punctuation errors to correct. For Sentence 1, write the capitalization and punctuation rule numbers for each correction in bold. For Sentence 2, write the capitalization and punctuation corrections. Use the capitalization and punctuation rule pages to help you.

1. **N**o, **I**'ve not been to **B**angor, **M**aine, in **A**pril for their white birch events**.**

   Editing Guide for Example 1 Sentence: Capitals: 5   Commas: 3   Apostrophes: 1   End Marks: 1

2. well lester my mothers oldest brother is a hermit

   Editing Guide for Example 2 Sentence: Capitals: 2   Commas: 3   Apostrophes: 1   End Marks: 1

Chapter 11, Lesson 1, Practice 1

Write the capitalization and punctuation rule numbers for each correction in bold.

700 **C**ollege **A**ve**.**

Bigelow**, S**outh **C**arolina 73086

May 4**,** 20__

Dear **A**licia**,**

Aunt **L**inda surprised me with two front row tickets to the concert at **W**allace **A**rena

on the first day of **J**une**. C**indy **M**artin and the **M**arletts will be performing**. Y**es**,** I know

you love their music**. T**hat is why **I** want you to take my other ticket**. I** hope you can make

the concert in **J**une**. W**rite back soon**.**

Your cousin**,**

Ashley

Editing Guide: Capitals: 24   Commas: 5   Periods: 1   End Marks: 6

Chapter 11, Lesson 2, Practice 1

Write the capitalization and punctuation corrections only.

504 west egg blvd

meadow lake montana 64900

september 16 20—

dear uncle charles

i heard about the honor you received at the indiana state highway police awards banquet

we are very proud of your achievement congratulations on such a high honor

your only nephew

collin

Editing Guide: Capitals: 21	Commas: 4	Periods: 1	End Marks: 3

Chapter 12, Lesson 3, Practice

Make corrections to the following paragraph.

Hiking in the woods can be full of suprises. There is all kinds of critters that rome the woods, everything from squirrels and snakes to turtels of various kinds one needs to be prepared for an host of eventualities. Also, many wildflowers grows in the shade of full-grown trees flowers such as bluets, jack-in-the-pulpit, and coral bells. Anyone looking for adventure can discover something knew each time he "hits the trail"

Total Mistakes: 12

Chapter 13, Lesson 1, Practice 1

On notebook paper, add the part that is underlined in the parentheses to make each fragment into a complete sentence.

1. Inside the shed behind the house   (subject part, predicate part, <u>both the subject and predicate</u>)

2. Slipped and slid on the snowy hillside   (<u>subject part</u>, predicate part, both the subject and predicate)

3. The unusually large painting in the foyer   (subject part, <u>predicate part</u>, both the subject and predicate)

Chapter 13, Lesson 1, Practice 2

Identify each kind of sentence by writing the abbreviation in the blank. (**S, F**).

_____ 1. The big hawk swooped toward the frightened mouse.

_____ 2. Summer squash ripened early.

_____ 3. Lying abandoned near the shore.

_____ 4. Interest skyrockets.

_____ 5. Weird noises.

Chapter 13, Lesson 2, Practice 1

Put a slash to separate each run-on sentence below. Then, correct the run-on sentences by rewriting them as indicated by the labels in parentheses at the end of each sentence.

1. The children were playing they were happy. (**SS**)

_____

2. The car is in the garage the bicycle is in the garage. (**SCS**)

_____

3. The boys washed the car they waxed the car. (**SCV**)

_____

Chapter 13, Lesson 2, Practice 2

Identify each kind of sentence by writing the abbreviation in the blank.
(**S, SS, F, SCS, SCV**)

_____ 1. Alongside the narrow road.

_____ 2. The faucet sprung a leak. Dad fixed it.

_____ 3. The astronauts put on their helmets and walked in space.

_____ 4. Mom lit all of the candles on the cake.

_____ 5. Parsley and marjoram are her favorite spices.

Chapter 13, Lesson 3, Practice 1

Put a slash to separate each run-on sentence below. Then, correct the run-on sentences by rewriting them as indicated by the labels in parentheses at the end of each sentence.

1. The disgruntled wrestler argued with the referee the referee would not change his mind. (**CD**, but)

_____

_____

2. The disgruntled wrestler argued with the referee the referee would not change his mind. (**CD**; however,)

_____

_____

3. The disgruntled wrestler argued with the referee he fought with the referee. (**SCV**)

_____

_____

4. The disgruntled wrestler argued with the referee the referee would not change his mind. (**CD**;)

_____

_____

Chapter 13, Lesson 3, Practice 2	Chapter 13, Lesson 3, Practice 3
Identify each kind of sentence by writing the abbreviation in the blank. (**S**, **F**, **SCS**, **SCV**, **CD**) _____ 1. The buzzard swooped and grabbed the kitten. _____ 2. Put into a defenseless position. _____ 3. Mom fixed the soup; Lori baked a pie. _____ 4. His warmth and kindness were appreciated.	On notebook paper, write three compound sentences using these labels to guide you: ① (**CD**, but) ② (**CD**; therefore,) ③ (**CD**;)

Chapter 14, Lesson 1, Practice 1

Put a slash to separate each run-on sentence below. Then, correct the run-on sentences by rewriting them as indicated by the labels in parentheses **( )** at the end of each sentence.

1. Dad unleashed the dog the cat took cover. (**CX**, when) (1)

_____

_____

2. Dad unleashed the dog the cat took cover. (**CX**, when) (2)

_____

_____

Chapter 14, Lesson 1, Practice 2

Identify each kind of sentence by writing the abbreviation in the blank. (**S**, **F**, **SCS**, **SCV**, **CD**, **CX**)

_____ 1. Because her cupboard was bare.

_____ 2. The traffic light did not work; however, there was a stop sign.

_____ 3. After the storm subsided, Joe returned home.

_____ 4. The phone quit ringing before I got to it.

_____ 5. The nearly voiceless cheerleaders jumped and shouted with joy.

_____ 6. We gave them warning, but they totally ignored us.

Chapter 14, Lesson 2, Practice 1

Put a slash to separate each run-on sentence below. Then, correct the run-on sentences by rewriting them as indicated by the labels in parentheses **( )** at the end of each sentence.

---

1. Dad unleashed the dog the cat took cover. (**CX**, after)(1)

_____

_____

2. Sue gathered the eggs she put on her sunbonnet. (**CX**, before)(1)

_____

_____

3. The little boy fell his shoelaces came untied. (**CX**, when)(2)

_____

_____

Chapter 14, Lesson 2, Practice 2

Identify each kind of sentence by writing the abbreviation in the blank. (**S, F, SCS, SCV, CD, CX**)

_____ 1. There was constant turmoil; consequently, we left.

_____ 2. Since the road was closed, we had to detour.

_____ 3. The boys and girls watched football yesterday.

_____ 4. Only because no one else had asked.

_____ 5. The water was nearly as high as the bridge.

_____ 6. We ran to the window before the rainbow disappeared.

_____ 7. Jeremy sat and twiddled his thumbs after dinner.

Chapter 14, Lesson 2, Practice 3

On a sheet of paper, write three complex sentences. Underline each <u>subordinate</u> sentence.

Chapter 14, Lesson 3, Practice 1

Put a slash to separate each run-on sentence below. Then, correct the run-on sentences by rewriting them as indicated by the labels in parentheses ( ) at the end of each sentence.

1. Mom opened the door the puppies ran outside. (**CX**, after) (1)

_____

_____

2. The tiny baby cried her bottle was empty. (**CX**, when) (2)

_____

_____

Chapter 14, Lesson 3, Practice 2

Identify each kind of sentence by writing the abbreviation in the blank. (**S, F, SCS, SCV, CD, CX**)

_____ 1. The storm passed through; however, we escaped injury.

_____ 2. When I balanced my checkbook, I heaved a sigh of relief.

_____ 3. He sometimes drove in the middle of the road to avoid the potholes.

_____ 4. The robins and mockingbirds declared war on each other.

_____ 5. Just as he crested the hill.

Chapter 14, Lesson 3, Practice 3

On a sheet of paper, write three complex sentences. Underline each <u>subordinate</u> sentence.

Chapter 14, Lesson 3, Practice 4

On a sheet of paper, write three compound sentences, using these labels to guide you:
1. (**CD**, but)
2. (**CD**; therefore,)
3. (**CD**;)

Chapter 15, Lesson 1, Practice

Part A: Underline each noun to be made possessive and write singular or plural (**S-P**), the rule number, and the possessive form. Part B: Write each noun as singular possessive and then as plural possessive.

1. For a singular noun - add ('s) Rule 1: boy's			2. For a plural noun that ends in *s* - add (') Rule 2: boys'		3. For a plural noun that does not end in *s* - add ('s) Rule 3: men's	
Part A	**S-P**	**Rule**	**Possessive Form**	**Part B**	**Singular Poss**	**Plural Poss**
1. wind velocity				5. egret		
2. donkeys tails				6. woman		
3. patients rights				7. pansy		
4. children pleas				8. wife		

Chapter 15, Lesson 2, Practice

Part A: Underline each noun to be made possessive and write singular or plural (**S-P**), the rule number, and the possessive form. Part B: Write each noun as singular possessive and then as plural possessive.

1. For a singular noun - add ('s) Rule 1: boy's			2. For a plural noun that ends in *s* - add (') Rule 2: boys'		3. For a plural noun that does not end in *s* - add ('s) Rule 3: men's	
Part A	**S-P**	**Rule**	**Possessive Form**	**Part B**	**Singular Poss**	**Plural Poss**
1. hens eggs				5. deer		
2. officer badge				6. angel		
3. tractor muffler				7. eel		
4. Arnold mother				8. child		

Chapter 15, Lesson 3, Practice

Part A: Underline each noun to be made possessive and write singular or plural (**S-P**), the rule number, and the possessive form. Part B: Write each noun as singular possessive and then as plural possessive.

1. For a singular noun - add ('s) Rule 1: boy's			2. For a plural noun that ends in *s* - add (') Rule 2: boys'		3. For a plural noun that does not end in *s* - add ('s) Rule 3: men's	
Part A	**S-P**	**Rule**	**Possessive Form**	**Part B**	**Singular Poss**	**Plural Poss**
1. jewelers rings				5. monkey		
2. pilot itinerary				6. wolf		
3. dogs fleas				7. ox		
4. Leo suitcase				8. blizzard		

Chapter 16, Lesson 3, Practice

For sentences 1-4, replace each underlined pronoun by writing the correct form in the first blank and **S** or **O** for subjective or objective case in the second blank.

1. <u>Us</u> volunteers were eager to help. _____ ____
2. Win a vacation from <u>we</u> ladies. _____ ____
3. Make a reservation for Mom and <u>they</u>. ____ ____
4. Mark and <u>us</u> will probably drive. _____ ___

Chapter 17, Lesson 1, Practice

Use the Quotation Rules to help punctuate the quotations below. Underline the explanatory words.

1. reverend simms remarked the time for forgiveness has come

2. the time for forgiveness has come reverend simms remarked

3. i whispered to patty before the christmas dance mind your manners

4. mind your manners i whispered to patty before the christmas dance

Chapter 17, Lesson 2, Practice 1

Use the Quotation Rules to help punctuate the quotations below. Underline the explanatory words.

1. look out the window lucy shouted

2. where can i reach you in memphis todd asked

3. head south she said into montgomery county

4. when i climbed pinnacle mountain she gasped i nearly fainted

5. albert inquired how far is albuquerque from here

6. sheila insisted your taxes are due tomorrow

Chapter 17, Lesson 2, Practice 2

On notebook paper, write three sentences demonstrating each of the three quotations: Beginning quote, end quote, and split quote.

Chapter 17, Lesson 3, Practice 1

Use the Quotation Rules to help punctuate the quotations below. Underline the explanatory words.

1. marsha did you see the aardvark at the zoo inquired bert

2. bert inquired marsha did you see the aardvark at the zoo

3. marsha bert inquired did you see the aardvark at the zoo

4. marsha did you see the aardvark at the zoo inquired bert i was hoping you got to pet it

---

Chapter 17, Lesson 3, Practice 2

On notebook paper, write three sentences demonstrating each of the three quotations: Beginning quote, end quote, and split quote.

Chapter 18 Lesson 1, Practice

Underline each verb or verb phrase. Identify the verb tense by writing a number **1** for present tense, a number **2** for past tense, or a number **3** for future tense. Write the past tense form and **R** or **I** for Regular or Irregular.

Verb Tense		Main Verb Past Tense Form	R or I
	1. Dad coughed all night long.		
	2. They are sitting in the parlor.		
	3. The boys have lost their tournament.		
	4. Dana will pretend she is ill.		
	5. They had jumped in icy water.		
	6. The birds were flying south.		
	7. Richard sleeps in his tent.		

Chapter 18, Lesson 2, Practice

Underline each verb or verb phrase. Identify the verb tense by writing a number **1** for present tense, a number **2** for past tense, or a number **3** for future tense. Write the past tense form and **R** or **I** for Regular or Irregular.

Verb Tense		Main Verb Past Tense Form	R or I
	1. She is driving to Kansas City.		
	2. Jack called from Alaska last night.		
	3. Barry has entered the seminary.		
	4. I will buy a new truck this summer.		
	5. We have eaten the whole watermelon.		
	6. She sings in the local choir.		
	7. He had twice interrupted the parade.		
	8. The fire is burning out of control.		
	9. The show will begin at 8:00.		

Chapter 18, Lesson 3, Practice 1

Underline each verb or verb phrase. Identify the verb tense by writing a number **1** for present tense, a number **2** for past tense, or a number **3** for future tense. Write the past tense form and **R** or **I** for Regular or Irregular.

Verb Tense		Main Verb Past Tense Form	R or I
	1. The clouds will be invading soon.		
	2. He is writing a novel.		
	3. Did you empty the trash?		
	4. Today, they are climbing the mountain.		

Chapter 18, Lesson 3, Practice 2

Change the underlined present tense verbs in Paragraph 1 to past tense verbs in Paragraph 2.

Paragraph 1: Present Tense

When somebody new **moves** into the neighborhood, my mom **greets** them with open arms. She **makes** them feel welcome with little effort. Her homemade coffeecake **is** always a big hit, of course, but her inviting smile **speaks** more than a thousand words. She **believes** in making newcomers feel welcome and **treats** them like family.

Paragraph 2: Past Tense

When somebody new _____ into the neighborhood, my mom _____ them with open arms. She _____ them feel welcome with little effort. Her homemade coffeecake _____ always a big hit, of course, but her inviting smile _____ more than a thousand words. She _____ in making newcomers feel welcome and _____ them like family.

Chapter 18, Lesson 3, Practice 3

Write the seven present tense helping verbs, the five past tense helping verbs, and the two future tense helping verbs on the lines below.

Present Tense Helping Verbs	Past Tense Helping Verbs	Future Tense Helping Verbs
_____	_____	_____
_____	_____	_____
_____	_____	
_____	_____	
_____	_____	
_____		
_____		

Chapter 18, Lesson 3, Practice 4

Change the underlined mixed tense verbs in Paragraph 1 to present tense verbs in Paragraph 2.

Paragraph 1: Mixed Tenses

Sometimes, I **took** my shoes off when I **waded** in the creek. The water **is** so invigorating. I **loved** to feel the ripples **pass** through my toes. On warm days, I **sit** on a rock in the middle of the creek and **felt** like I **was** in heaven.

Paragraph 2: Present Tense

Sometimes, I _____ my shoes off when I _____ in the creek. The water _____ so invigorating. I _____ to feel the ripples _____ through my toes. On warm days, I _____ on a rock in the middle of the creek and _____ like I _____ in heaven.

Chapter 19, Lesson 3, Practice:

Copy the following words on notebook paper. Write the correct contraction beside each word.

Words: cannot, let us, do not, was not, they are, are not, had not, is not, she is, who is, you are, did not, it is, we are, were not, does not, has not, I am, I have, I had, will not, I will, would not, I would, should not, could not, they would

Chapter 20, Lesson 1, Practice 1

Write the rule numbers and the different forms for the adjectives below. For irregular forms write **Irr**.

Comparative: Rule 1: Use **-er** with 1 or 2 syllable words and **more** with -ful words, awkward words, or words with 3 or more syllables.

Superlative: Rule 2: Use **-est** with 1 or 2 syllable words and **most** with -ful words, awkward words, or words with 3 or more syllables.

Simple Adjective Form	Rule Box	Comparative Adjective Form	Rule Box	Superlative Adjective Form
1. easy				
2. turbulent				
3. little				
4. fair				
5. gracious				
6. much				
7. eager				

Chapter 20, Lesson 1, Practice 2

In each blank, write the correct form of the adjective in parentheses to complete the sentences.

1. Eric's training was _____ than Brian's. (extensive)

2. Your answer is _____ than the one in the book. (good)

3. He is a _____ candidate than his brother. (worthy)

4. John is never anything but _____. (kind)

5. Lance bought the _____ diamond in the store. (expensive)

Chapter 20, Lesson 2, Practice 1

Underline the negative words in each sentence. Rewrite each sentence and correct the double negative mistake as indicated by the rule number in parentheses at the end of the sentence.

Rule 1	Rule 2	Rule 3
Change the second negative to a positive.	Take out the negative part of a contraction.	Remove the first negative word (verb change).

1. She couldn't see nothing in the distance. (Rule 1)

2. He doesn't have no common sense. (Rule 3)

3. She hasn't never stayed home alone. (Rule 2)

4. Sue doesn't never come home for Christmas. (Rule 1)

5. There isn't no right answer. (Rule 2)

6. I didn't find nothing in that desk. (Rule 3)

7. Joe hadn't never fried eggs before. (Rule 2)

8. She hasn't eaten no lunch today. (Rule 1)

Chapter 20, Lesson 2, Practice 2

On notebook paper, make a list of fifteen contractions, then write the words from which the contractions come.

Chapter 20, Lesson 3, Practice 1

Underline the negative words in each sentence. Rewrite each sentence and correct the double negative mistake as indicated by the rule number in parentheses at the end of the sentence.

Rule 1	Rule 2	Rule 3
Change the second negative to a positive.	Take out the negative part of a contraction.	Remove the first negative word (verb change).

1. Kay didn't insist on nothing today. (Rule 1)

2. She wasn't never inconsiderate. (Rule 2)

3. He wouldn't ask no one for a pen. (Rule 1)

4. Kevin hadn't never milked a cow. (Rule 3)

5. Nancy hadn't never traveled overseas. (Rule 2)

6. He doesn't never wear shoes in the summer. (Rule 3)

7. The judge didn't want no flimsy excuses. (Rule 1)

8. The applicant didn't want no special privileges. (Rule 3)

Chapter 20, Lesson 3, Practice 2

On notebook paper, write three sentences in which you demonstrate each of the double negative rules above. Underline the negative word in each sentence.

Chapter 20, Lesson 3, Practice 3

Write the rule numbers and the different forms for the adjectives below. For irregular forms, write **Irr**.

Comparative: Rule 1: Use **-er** with 1 or 2 syllable words and **more** with -ful words, awkward words, or words with 3 or more syllables.

Superlative: Rule 2: Use **-est** with 1 or 2 syllable words and **most** with -ful words, awkward words, or words with 3 or more syllables.

Simple Adjective Form	Rule Box	Comparative Adjective Form	Rule Box	Superlative Adjective Form
1. vocal				
2. well				
3. painful				
4. vicious				
5. smart				
6. ill				
7. wise				

Chapter 20, Lesson 3, Practice 4

On notebook paper, write three sentences, demonstrating each of the three degrees of adjectives. Identify the form you used by writing **simple**, **comparative**, or **superlative** at the end of each sentence.

Chapter 20, Lesson 3, Practice 5

In each blank, write the correct form of the adjective in parentheses to complete the sentences.

1. Troy is the _____ player on the team. (impatient)

2. Roy has a very _____ personality. (outgoing)

3. Those were the _____ pancakes I'd ever tasted. (good)

4. These pretzels are _____ than those chips. (salty)

5. She is the _____resident on the street. (vigilant)

Chapter 20, Lesson 3, Practice 6

On a notebook paper, make a list of ten contractions, then write the words from which the contractions come.

Chapter 21, Lesson 1, Practice

Choose an answer from the pronoun choices in parentheses. Fill in the other columns according to the titles. (**S** or **P** stands for singular or plural.)

Pronoun-antecedent agreement

1. The bride looked at (her, their) mother.

2. Dad will call at (his, their) convenience.

3. Margie tripped on (her, their) shoelaces.

4. The raccoons crowded back into (its, their) den.

5. My aunts got lost on (her, their) trip.

Pronoun Choice	S or P	Antecedent	S or P

Chapter 21, Lesson 2, Practice

Choose an answer from the choices in parentheses. Fill in the other columns according to the titles.
(**S** or **P** stands for singular or plural.)

Pronoun-antecedent agreement

1. One member of the band dropped (his, their) oboe.

2. The antiques had no prices on (it, them).

3. The senator offered (his, their) resignation.

4. The trainees raised (his/her, their) hands.

5. The farmer wrapped (his, their) bales of hay.

6. The postman made (his, their) rounds early.

Pronoun Choice	S or P	Antecedent	S or P

Chapter 21, Lesson 3, Practice

Choose an answer from the choices in parentheses. Fill in the other columns according to the titles.
(**S** or **P** stands for singular or plural.)

Pronoun-antecedent agreement

1. The players misplaced (his, their) helmets.

2. Something in the hole stuck (its, their) tongue out.

3. The pilots got (its, their) way at contract time.

4. The comedian displayed (his, their) natural wit.

5. My sister lost (her, their) bracelet at the zoo.

6. The lobster attacked with (its, their) claws.

7. The soldiers lost (his/her, their) way.

8. My mattress has lost (its, their) firmness.

9. The deacon gave (his, their) testimony.

10. Azaleas in the side yard lost (its, their) luster.

Pronoun Choice	S or P	Antecedent	S or P

Chapter 22, Lesson 2, Practice

Underline each subject and fill in each column according to the title.

	List each Verb	Write PrN, PA, or None	Write L or A
1. Grapes are expensive.			
2. Those details are important.			
3. His passport is lost.			
4. We ate at the diner today.			
5. Hawaii is our fiftieth state.			
6. Patience is a virtue.			
7. The answer is too vague.			
8. I called him late last night.			
9. We left the car at the airport.			
10. Toby was totally surprised.			
11. Aspirin relieved his headache.			
12. The judges were clearly impartial.			
13. She painted the foyer gold.			
14. He believes in ghosts.			
15. Charlie is my hero.			

Chapter 22, Lesson 3, Practice 1

Write the rule numbers from Reference 66 and the correct plural form of the nouns below.

		Rule	Plural Form			Rule	Plural Form
1.	donkey			6.	monopoly		
2.	wolf			7.	fish		
3.	tax			8.	barnacle		
4.	ox			9.	reef		
5.	tornado			10.	monkey		

Chapter 22, Lesson 3, Practice 2

On notebook paper, make a list of ten contractions, then write the words from which the contractions come.

Chapter 22, Lesson 3, Practice 3

Underline each subject and fill in each column according to the title.

1. Kiwis are delicious.

2. Kent drove to the lake.

3. Warren is president this year.

4. Menacing crows ravaged the corn crop.

5. Her address is incorrect.

6. His parents are reporters.

List each Verb	Write PrN, PA, or None	Write L or A

Chapter 23, Lesson 1, Practice

Use butcher paper, large pieces of construction paper, or poster board to make a colorful wall poster identifying the five parts of a friendly letter and the parts of an envelope. Write the title and an example for each of the five parts. Illustrate your work. Then, give an oral presentation about the friendly letter and the envelope when you have finished.

Chapter 23, Lesson 2, Practice

Write a friendly letter to a special friend or relative. Before you start, review the references and tips for writing friendly letters. After your letter has been edited, fold the letter and put it in an envelope. Address the envelope properly and mail it. Don't forget the stamp. (*E-mail does not take the place of this assignment.*)

Chapter 23, Lesson 3, Practice 1

On notebook paper, identify the parts of a friendly letter and envelope by writing the titles and an example for each title.

Chapter 23, Lesson 3, Practice 2

Write a friendly letter to a neighbor, nursing home resident, or relative. This person must be someone that is different from the person chosen in the previous lesson. Before you start, review the references and tips for writing friendly letters. After your letter has been edited, fold the letter and put it in an envelope. Address the envelope properly and mail it. Don't forget the stamp.

Chapter 24, Lesson 1, Practice

Using butcher paper, large pieces of construction paper, or poster board, make a colorful wall poster, identifying the six parts of a business letter and the parts of a business envelope. Write the title and an example for each of the parts of the business letter and envelope. Illustrate your work. Then, give an oral presentation about the business letter and the envelope when you have finished.

Chapter 24, Lesson 2, Practice

Write a friendly letter to a special friend or relative. Before you start, review the references and tips for writing friendly letters. After your letter has been edited, fold the letter and put it in an envelope. Address the envelope properly and mail it. Don't forget the stamp.

Chapter 24, Lesson 3, Practice 1

On notebook paper, identify the parts of a business letter and envelope by writing the titles and an example for each title. Use References 70 and 71 to help you.

Chapter 24, Lesson 3, Practice 2

Write a business letter. You may invent the company and the situation for which you are writing. Before you begin, review the reasons for writing business letters and the four types of business letters *(Reference 69 on page 46)*. After your letter has been edited, fold the letter and put it in an envelope. Address the envelope properly.

Chapter 25, Lesson 1, Practice

Write your own thank-you note. First, think of a person who has done something nice for you or has given you a gift *(even the gift of time)*. Next, write that person a thank-you note using the information in the Reference section as a guide.

Chapter 25, Lesson 2, Practice

Make your own invitation card. First, think of a special event or occasion and who will be invited. Next, make an invitation to send out using the information in the Reference section as a guide. Illustrate your card appropriately.

Chapter 25, Lesson 3, Practice 1

Write another thank-you note. First, think of a person who has done something nice for you or has given you a gift *(even the gift of time)*. Next, write that person a thank-you note using the information in the Reference section as a guide.

Chapter 25, Lesson 3, Practice 2

Make another invitation card. First, think of a special event or occasion and who will be invited. Next, make an invitation to send out using the information in the Reference section as a guide. Illustrate your card appropriately.

Chapter 26, Lesson 2, Practice 1

Match each part of a book listed below with the type of information it may give you. Write the appropriate letter in the blank. You may use a letter only once.

A. Title page   B. Copyright page   C. Index   D. Bibliography   E. Appendix   F. Glossary

1. _____ A list of books used by the author as references

2. _____ ISBN number

3. _____ Used to locate topics quickly

Chapter 26, Lesson 2, Practice 2

Match each part of a book listed below with the type of information it may give you. Write the appropriate letter in the blank. You may use a letter only once.

A. Title page   B. Table of contents   C. Copyright page   D. Index   E. Bibliography
F. Preface   G. Body

1. _____ Exact page numbers for a particular topic

2. _____ Text of the book

3. _____ Reason the book was written

4. _____ Books listed for finding more information

Chapter 26, Lesson 2, Practice 3

On notebook paper, write the nine parts of a book and label them front or back.

Chapter 26, Lesson 3, Practice 1

Write the nine parts of a book on a poster and write a description beside each part. Illustrate and color the nine parts.

Chapter 26, Lesson 3, Practice 2

Underline each subject and fill in each column according to the title.

	List each Verb	Write PrN, PA, or None	Write L or A
1. Grapefruits are healthy.			
2. His decision was final.			
3. My cousin paid the bill.			
4. Greenland is a remote island.			
5. Most parents are wise.			
6. She sometimes sleeps in church.			
7. The platypus is a shrewd hunter.			
8. The interstate is a dangerous road.			
9. Spelunkers are modern-day explorers.			
10. Plagiarism is a violation of the law.			

Chapter 27, Lesson 1, Practice 1

Underline the correct answer.

1. The type of reference book that is published annually is the

   (atlas,   dictionary,   almanac,   encyclopedia).

2. Maps of rivers, lakes, oceans, and continents are the principal contents of

   (a dictionary,   an atlas,   an encyclopedia,   an almanac).

3. The type of catalog card one should check if he/she does not know an author's name or the title

   of a book is (a wild card,   a subject card,   a trump card,   a fragment card).

4. The number in the upper left-hand corner of a catalog card is called the

   (press number,   copyright number,   page number,   call number).

5. Nonfiction books are arranged on the shelves in (numerical,   alphabetical) order.

Chapter 27, Lesson 1, Practice 2

Write True or False in the blank.

1. _____ The first line of information on a title card and subject card is the same.

2. _____ Biographies are arranged on the shelves by authors' last names.

3. _____ The Readers' Guide to Periodical Literature is an index to biographies of contemporary Americans.

4. _____ Pronunciations and origins of words are contained in dictionary entries.

5. _____ Fiction books are arranged alphabetically by authors' last names.

Chapter 27, Lesson 1, Practice 3

Select eight of your favorite fiction books and alphabetize them by the authors' last names.

Chapter 27, Lesson 1, Practice 4

Draw and label the three catalog cards for this book on a sheet of notebook paper: 850.6 *Lyrics and Lyres* by Jill Criswell, Bluffton Press, Erie, 1997, 262 p.

Chapter 27, Lesson 2, Practice

Using the index of a science *(or other subject)* book, write ten things that the index could help you answer quickly and the pages where the answers are found.

Chapter 27, Lesson 3, Practice

Use the Table of Contents example in Reference 77 to answer the questions below.

1. What is the title of the chapter that would tell you how a trucker recovers at the end of a long day on the road?

   _____

2. On what page does chapter 2 end?

   _____

3. In what chapter would you find information about the qualities needed to be a trucker?

   _____

4. On what page does chapter 4 start?

   _____

Chapter 28, Lesson 1, Practice
Give an oral report on parallel forms for outlines. Make an outline as a visual aid to help in your presentation. Include different parallel forms in your outline. You may use the discussion points on parallel forms that are listed below. (*You may also use Reference 79 as your guide.*)

1. Explain that parallel form means using the same type of words to start each division of your outline.

2. Discuss how you can start each section with all nouns, all verbs, all prepositions, adjectives in front of nouns, etc.

3. Discuss how you used parallel form in each section of your outline.

4. Each new section can have a different parallel form. Explain that it doesn't matter how each section begins, it is just important to make sure each section has the same parallel form.

Chapter 28, Lesson 2, Practice
Copy the notes below into a two-point outline. Change wording to put notes into correct parallel form.

Notes	Outline
types of camping-out	
in a tent	
magic of night sounds	
starry nights	
motel	
voices in adjacent rooms	
ceiling lights	

Chapter 28, Lesson 3, Practice
Copy the notes below into a three-point outline. Change wording to put notes into correct parallel form.

Notes	Outline
kinds of gardens **vegetable gardens** that grow above ground underground **flowers** perennial varieties annuals **herbs** from seeds root sprouts	

Notes

TEST

SECTION

Chapter 2 Test

Exercise 1: Put the end marks and the abbreviations for each kind of sentence in the blanks below.

1. Did you sing in the choir _____

2. My sister started a new job _____

3. The lion ran toward the little girl _____

4. Wash the dishes in the sink _____

5. Did Keith meet the president _____

6. I ran the marathon with my friends _____

7. Dust the top shelf _____

8. I won the trip to Europe _____

Exercise 2: On a separate sheet of paper, write a sentence to demonstrate each of these four kinds of sentences: (1) Declarative (2) Interrogative (3) Exclamatory (4) Imperative. Write the correct punctuation and the abbreviation that identifies it at the end. Use these abbreviations: **D, Int, E, Imp.**

Exercise 3: Match the definitions. Write the correct letter beside each numbered concept.

_____	1. tells what the subject does	A.	verb, adjective, or adverb
_____	2. a/an are also called	B.	what?
_____	3. adjective modifies	C.	what is being said about?
_____	4. verb question	D.	person, place, or thing
_____	5. a definite article	E.	indefinite articles
_____	6. subject-noun question (thing)	F.	period
_____	7. article adjective can be called	G.	noun marker
_____	8. makes a request or gives a command	H.	who?
_____	9. noun	I.	noun or pronoun
_____	10. subject-noun question (person)	J.	the
_____	11. punctuation for declarative	K.	verb
_____	12. adverb modifies	L.	imperative sentence

Exercise 4: Identify each pair of words as synonyms or antonyms by putting parentheses ( ) around **syn** or **ant**.

1. bequeath, withhold	syn	ant	3. false, authentic	syn	ant
2. pardon, amnesty	syn	ant	4. acknowledge, admit	syn	ant

Exercise 5: Write a pair of synonyms beside number 1. Write a pair of antonyms beside number 2.

1. _____   2. _____

Exercise 6: In your journal, write a paragraph summarizing what you have learned this week.

Chapter 3 Test

Exercise 1: Classify each sentence.

1. _____ The tired, hungry campers hiked wearily.

2. _____ The three frightened deer quickly ran away.

3. _____ The brave young soldier turned swiftly around.

Exercise 2: Use Sentence 3 to underline the complete subject once and the complete predicate twice and to complete the table below.

List the Noun Used	List the Noun Job	Singular or Plural	Common or Proper	Simple Subject	Simple Predicate
1.	2.	3.	4.	5.	6.

Exercise 3: Name the four parts of speech that you have studied so far.

1. _____   2. _____   3. _____   4. _____

Exercise 4: Finding One Part of Speech. For each sentence, write **SN** above the simple subject and **V** above the simple predicate. Underline the word(s) for the part of speech listed to the left of each sentence.

Adjective(s):   1. The old couple slowly strolled along.

Adverb(s):   2. The children merrily played outside yesterday.

Noun(s):   3. The small toddler toppled over.

Adjective(s):   4. The chickens clucked loudly.

Verb(s):   5. The hero acted very bravely.

Adverb(s):   6. The bright balloons sagged sadly today.

Exercise 5: Identify each pair of words as synonyms or antonyms by putting parentheses ( ) around **syn** or **ant**.

1. argue, debate	syn	ant	5. destroy, abolish	syn	ant	9. acknowledge, admit	syn	ant
2. authentic, false	syn	ant	6. timid, audacious	syn	ant	10. conceal, exhume	syn	ant
3. prodigy, genius	syn	ant	7. pardon, amnesty	syn	ant	11. construction, dilapidation	syn	ant
4. fact, hypothesis	syn	ant	8. mimic, imitate	syn	ant	12. withhold, bequeath	syn	ant

Exercise 6: In your journal, write a paragraph summarizing what you have learned this week.

Chapter 4 Test

Exercise 1: Classify each sentence.

1. _____ Yesterday, the sleek black corvette stopped quite abruptly.

2. _____ The tired baby wailed impatiently today.

3. _____ The weary hikers trudged miserably home.

Exercise 2: Use Sentence 2 to underline the complete subject once and the complete predicate twice and to complete the table below.

List the Noun Used	List the Noun Job	Singular or Plural	Common or Proper	Simple Subject	Simple Predicate
1.	2.	3.	4.	5.	6.

Exercise 3: Name the four parts of speech that you have studied so far.

1. _____ 2. _____ 3. _____ 4. _____

Exercise 4: For each sentence, write the subject, then write **S** if the subject is singular or **P** if the subject is plural, write the rule number, and underline the correct verb in the sentence.

Rule 1: A singular subject must use a singular verb form that ends in **s**: *is, was, has, does,* or verbs ending with **s** or **es**.
Rule 2: A plural subject, a compound subject, or the subject **YOU** must use a plural verb form that has **no s** ending: *are, were, do, have,* or verbs without **s** or **es** endings. (A plural verb form is also called the *plain form.*)

Subject	S or P	Rule

1. Some snails (has, have) long antenna.
2. This tablecloth (wrinkle, wrinkles) too easily.
3. (Do, Does) the hikers ever get lost?
4. You (has, have) a legitimate argument.
5. The candle (is, are) painfully dim.
6. My shoes (was, were) too tight.
7. The mayor (has, have) rescheduled the meeting.
8. Tiffany and Glen (was, were) twins.
9. (Was, Were) your computer new or used?
10. The salamander (do, does) not seem tired.
11. One elephant (was, were) terribly stubborn.
12. The calendar (has, have) a missing month.

Exercise 5: Identify each pair of words as synonyms or antonyms by putting parentheses ( ) around **syn** or **ant**.

1. void, vacant	syn ant	5. conceal, exhume	syn ant	9. debate, argue	syn ant
2. false, authentic	syn ant	6. deception, fraud	syn ant	10. acknowledge, admit	syn ant
3. fact, hypothesis	syn ant	7. coherent, ramble	syn ant	11. audacious, timid	syn ant
4. prodigy, genius	syn ant	8. abolish, destroy	syn ant	12. competitor, colleague	syn ant

Exercise 6: In your journal, write a paragraph summarizing what you have learned this week.

Chapter 5 Test

Exercise 1: Classify each sentence.

1. _____ After the game, the spectators moved onto the basketball court.

2. _____ The fascinated child quickly rushed for the drifting bubbles.

3. _____ Eight mighty Olympians dashed briskly toward the finish line!

Exercise 2: Use Sentence 3 to underline the complete subject once and the complete predicate twice and to complete the table below.

List the Noun Used	List the Noun Job	Singular or Plural	Common or Proper	Simple Subject	Simple Predicate
1.	2.	3.	4.	5.	6.
7.	8.	9.	10.		

Exercise 3: Name the five parts of speech that you have studied so far.

1. _____ 2. _____ 3. _____ 4. _____ 5. _____

Exercise 4: Identify each pair of words as synonyms or antonyms by putting parentheses ( ) around *syn* or *ant*.

1. authentic, false	syn ant	5. ramble, coherent	syn ant	9. alliance, division	syn ant
2. frugal, thrifty	syn ant	6. conceal, exhume	syn ant	10. construction, dilapidation	syn ant
3. fraud, deception	syn ant	7. hateful, odious	syn ant	11. mimic, imitate	syn ant
4. destroy, abolish	syn ant	8. pardon, amnesty	syn ant	12. melodramatic, subdued	syn ant

Exercise 5: For each sentence, write the subject, then write **S** if the subject is singular or **P** if the subject is plural, write the rule number, and underline the correct verb in the sentence.

Rule 1: A singular subject must use a singular verb form that ends in **s**: *is, was, has, does, or verbs ending with* **s** *or* **es**.
Rule 2: A plural subject, a compound subject, or the subject **YOU** must use a plural verb form that has **no s** ending: *are, were, do, have, or verbs without* **s** *or* **es** *endings.* (A plural verb form is also called the *plain form*.)

Subject	S or P	Rule

1. Jessica and Jason (talk, talks) on the phone for hours.
2. The keys (was, were) locked in the car.
3. The boys (runs, run) to catch the frisbee.
4. Our parents (was, were) talking about the plans.
5. My car (look, looks) very dirty.
6. Your toothbrush and comb (is, are) in my drawer.
7. The kitten (was, were) licking its paws.
8. (Was, Were) Mom pleased with your grade?
9. Gloria and Wendi (is, are) going to the mall.
10. The company (has, have) many good employees.

Exercise 6: In your journal, write a paragraph summarizing what you have learned this week.

Chapter 6 Test

Exercise 1: Classify each sentence.

1. _____ She quietly walked through the dark hallway in the castle.

2. _____ They prayed daily for our country.

3. _____ Eat very slowly in the cafeteria.

Exercise 2: Use Sentence 1 to underline the complete subject once and the complete predicate twice and to complete the table below.

List the Noun Used	List the Noun Job	Singular or Plural	Common or Proper	Simple Subject	Simple Predicate
1.	2.	3.	4.	5.	6.
7.	8.	9.	10.		

Exercise 3: Name the six parts of speech that you have studied so far.

1. _____   2. _____   3. _____   4. _____   5. _____   6. _____

Exercise 4: Identify each pair of words as synonyms or antonyms by putting parentheses ( ) around **syn** or **ant**.

1. frugal, thrifty	syn ant	5. hateful, odious	syn ant	9. vacant, void	syn ant
2. alliance, division	syn ant	6. perpetual, constant	syn ant	10. veritable, fictitious	syn ant
3. prodigy, genius	syn ant	7. pardon, amnesty	syn ant	11. prodigal, wasteful	syn ant
4. ethical, carnal	syn ant	8. withhold, bequeath	syn ant	12. fraud, deception	syn ant

Exercise 5: For each sentence, write the subject, then write **S** if the subject is singular or **P** if the subject is plural, write the rule number, and underline the correct verb in the sentence.

Rule 1: A singular subject must use a singular verb form that ends in **s**: *is, was, has, does, or verbs ending with* **s** *or* **es**.
Rule 2: A plural subject, a compound subject, or the subject **YOU** must use a plural verb form that has **no s** ending: *are, were, do, have, or verbs without* **s** *or* **es** *endings.* (A plural verb form is also called the *plain form*.)

Subject	S or P	Rule

1. The tree (was, were) a beautiful specimen.
2. Chris and Shawna (is, are) staying in Oxford.
3. The stores (has, have) great holiday sales.
4. That puppy (need, needs) some food.
5. The flowers (is, are) very beautifully arranged.
6. My sister (was, were) taken to the hospital.
7. The food (is, are) in the lower cabinet.
8. (Do, Does) those students have the homework?
9. The painting (seem, seems) to be missing.
10. The boys (was, were) enjoying their vacation.

Exercise 6: On notebook paper, write as many prepositions as you can.

Exercise 7: In your journal, write a paragraph summarizing what you have learned this week.

Chapter 7 Test

Exercise 1: Classify each sentence.

1. _____ Yesterday, the assassin's airplane crashed directly into the president's headquarters!

2. _____ During biology class, we reviewed endlessly for our upcoming lab test.

3. _____ Drive very carefully around the sharp curves.

Exercise 2: Use Sentence 1 to underline the complete subject once and the complete predicate twice and to complete the table below.

List the Noun Used	List the Noun Job	Singular or Plural	Common or Proper	Simple Subject	Simple Predicate
1.	2.	3.	4.	5.	6.
7.	8.	9.	10.		

Exercise 3: Name the six parts of speech that you have studied so far.

1. _____ 2. _____ 3. _____ 4. _____ 5. _____ 6. _____

Exercise 4: Identify each pair of words as synonyms or antonyms by putting parentheses ( ) around *syn* or *ant*.

1. carnal, ethical	syn	ant	4. fictitious, veritable	syn	ant	7. proverbial, notorious	syn	ant
2. vague, specific	syn	ant	5. prodigal, wasteful	syn	ant	8. colleague, competitor	syn	ant
3. frivolous, grave	syn	ant	6. perpetual, constant	syn	ant	9. transparent, translucent	syn	ant

Exercise 5: Finding One Part of Speech. For each sentence, write **SN** above the simple subject and **V** above the simple predicate. Underline the word(s) for the part of speech listed to the left of each sentence.

Adjective(s): 1. Several mallard ducks landed in my grandfather's reflection pond.

Preposition(s): 2. I always jog in the park during the summer.

Pronoun(s): 3. My family and I cheered loudly for Steven from our seats in the stands.

Exercise 6: For each sentence, write the subject, then write **S** if the subject is singular or **P** if the subject is plural, write the rule number (Rule 1 for singular and Rule 2 for plural), and underline the correct verb in the sentence.

Subject	S or P	Rule

1. Those stories (sound, sounds) quite interesting.
2. Dustin and his girlfriend (is, are) flying to Denver.
3. The sun (was, were) shining.
4. You (was, were) great at playing the trombone.
5. (Does, Do) your dog bite?
6. (Doesn't, Don't) your parents wonder where you are?
7. My friend (live, lives) in another country.
8. Those clothes in the basket (was, were) dirty.

Exercise 7: On notebook paper, write seven subject pronouns, seven possessive pronouns, and seven object pronouns.

Exercise 8: In your journal, write a paragraph summarizing what you have learned this week.

Chapter 8 Test

Exercise 1: Classify each sentence.

1. _____ Did the lead dancer fall across the stage during the spring musical?

2. _____ The big flock of turkeys could be seen from our balcony window.

3. _____ The frightened rabbit did not dash immediately for cover.

Exercise 2: Use Sentence 2 to underline the complete subject once and the complete predicate twice and to complete the table below.

List the Noun Used	List the Noun Job	Singular or Plural	Common or Proper	Simple Subject	Simple Predicate
1.	2.	3.	4.	5.	6.
7.	8.	9.	10.		
11.	12.	13.	14.		

Exercise 3: Name the six parts of speech that you have studied so far.

1. _____ 2. _____ 3. _____ 4. _____ 5. _____ 6. _____

Exercise 4: For each sentence, write the subject, then write **S** if the subject is singular or **P** if the subject is plural, write the rule number (Rule 1 for singular and Rule 2 for plural), and underline the correct verb in the sentence.

Subject	S or P	Rule

1. My sister (look, looks) beautiful today.
2. Pictures (was, were) taken of the crime scene.
3. (Do, Does) these clothes belong on the floor?
4. The posters (was, were) left in my car.
5. Our team (is, are) playing right now.
6. You (has, have) four dollars left.
7. Megan and Dylan (has, have) fed the dog.

Exercise 5: Finding One Part of Speech. For each sentence, write **SN** above the simple subject and **V** (or **HV** and **V**) above the simple predicate. Underline the word(s) for the part of speech listed to the left of each sentence.

Preposition(s): 1. The administrators of the school district gather for the first meeting of the year.

Verb(s): 2. During the winter, we are driving to Lake Tahoe for our vacation.

Pronoun(s): 3. He is not staying with our family this year.

Exercise 6: Identify each pair of words as synonyms or antonyms by putting parentheses ( ) around **syn** or **ant**.

1. void, vacant	syn ant	5. veracity, truth	syn ant	9. condense, abbreviate	syn ant
2. debate, argue	syn ant	6. frivolous, grave	syn ant	10. proverbial, notorious	syn ant
3. myth, fact	syn ant	7. mimic, imitate	syn ant	11. melodramatic, subdued	syn ant
4. vague, specific	syn ant	8. ethical, carnal	syn ant	12. spurious, accurate	syn ant

Exercise 7: In your journal, write a paragraph summarizing what you have learned this week.

Chapter 9 Test

Exercise 1: Classify each sentence.

1. _____ The city manager and his assistant wrestled with several fresh alternatives.

2. _____ Do not drive across the flooded highway after a big rain in the spring.

3. _____ Did the old swaybacked mare collapse unexpectedly during the charity horse race?

Exercise 2: Use Sentence 2 to underline the complete subject once and the complete predicate twice and to complete the table below.

List the Noun Used	List the Noun Job	Singular or Plural	Common or Proper	Simple Subject	Simple Predicate
1.	2.	3.	4.	5.	6.
7.	8.	9.	10.		
11.	12.	13.	14.		

Exercise 3: Name the eight parts of speech that you have studied.

1._____ 2._____ 3._____ 4._____ 5._____ 6._____ 7._____ 8._____

Exercise 4: Answer each question below on a sheet of notebook paper.

1. List the 8 **be** verbs.
2. What are the parts of a verb phrase?
3. Name the seven subject pronouns.
4. Name the seven possessive pronouns.
5. Name the seven object pronouns.
6. What part of speech is the word NOT?

Exercise 5: Identify each pair of words as synonyms or antonyms by putting parentheses ( ) around **syn** or **ant**.

1. odd, quaint	syn ant	5. veracity, truth	syn ant	9. honesty, integrity	syn ant
2. vague, specific	syn ant	6. spurious, accurate	syn ant	10. simultaneous, periodic	syn ant
3. fact, myth	syn ant	7. savory, bland	syn ant	11. condense, abbreviate	syn ant
4. odious, hateful	syn ant	8. fraud, deception	syn ant	12. transparent, translucent	syn ant

Exercise 6: Underline the correct homonym in each sentence.

1. When I finished the race, I was pathetically (weak, week).
2. There are no (capital, capitol) letters in common nouns.
3. The priest (lead, led) his parishioners on a religious pilgrimage.
4. Janet said (their, they're) still planning to go.
5. Be sure to type your reply on letterhead (stationary, stationery).
6. He (knew, new) better than to ask me that question.
7. Together, they set (forth, fourth) on a new crusade.
8. Ethiopia has not seen (piece, peace) in years.

Exercise 7: In your journal, write a paragraph summarizing what you have learned this week.

Chapter 10 Test

Exercise 1: Classify each sentence.

1. _____ The teakettle on the wood stove grated on Mom's nerves during her naptime.

2. _____ Whew! My goldfish landed in the kitchen sink!

3. _____ The excited toddler was eagerly running after the balloon and was squealing delightedly during the chase.

Exercise 2: Use Sentence 3 to underline the complete subject once and the complete predicate twice and to complete the table below.

List the Noun Used	List the Noun Job	Singular or Plural	Common or Proper	Simple Subject	Simple Predicate
1.	2.	3.	4.	5.	6.
7.	8.	9.	10.		
11.	12.	13.	14.		

Exercise 3: Name the eight parts of speech that you have studied.

1. _____ 2. _____ 3. _____ 4. _____ 5. _____ 6. _____ 7. _____ 8. _____

Exercise 4: Identify each pair of words as synonyms or antonyms by putting parentheses ( ) around **syn** or **ant**.

1. burn, smolder	syn ant	5. frugal, thrifty	syn ant	9. acknowledge, admit	syn ant
2. bland, savory	syn ant	6. conceal, exhume	syn ant	10. honesty, integrity	syn ant
3. timid, audacious	syn ant	7. amiable, repulsive	syn ant	11. spontaneous, forced	syn ant
4. odd, quaint	syn ant	8. escalate, expand	syn ant	12. periodic, simultaneous	syn ant

Exercise 5: Underline the correct homonym in each sentence.

1. Melissa looked at Chris and shook her head (no, know).
2. I bought a (knew, new) pair of shoes yesterday.
3. Steven already (knew, new) the answer to the question.
4. You will make a (write, right) turn after you pass the blue house.
5. The flower's fresh (cent, scent) filled the room.
6. Mom (sent, cent) Kyle to his room.
7. I (know, no) that tomorrow is your birthday.
8. Don't forget to (right, write) your grandmother a thank-you note.

Exercise 6: Use the Editing Guide below each sentence to know how many capitalization and punctuation errors to correct. For Sentence 1, write the capitalization and punctuation rule numbers for each correction in bold. For Sentence 2, write the capitalization and punctuation corrections. Use the capitalization and punctuation rule pages to help you.

1. **D**id you know that **Dr. S**peer has been teaching at **E**astern **T**echnical **C**ollege since **A**ugust 12**, 1972?**

   Editing Guide: Capitals: 7   Commas: 1   Periods: 1   Apostrophes: 0   End Marks: 1

2. our trip to honduras was so successful that dr baker said he would take another group this july

   Editing Guide: Capitals: 5   Commas: 0   Periods: 1   Apostrophes: 0   End Marks: 1

Exercise 7: In your journal, write a paragraph summarizing what you have learned this week.

Chapter 11 Test A

Exercise 1: Sentence: Write the capitalization and punctuation rule numbers for each correction in bold.

1. **M**y teacher**, Ms. E.L. S**ummers**,** won the **Caldecott A**ward for her story <u>**T**hanksgiving **B**lessings</u>**.**

Editing Guide:	Capitals: 9	Commas: 2	Periods: 3	End Marks: 1	Underlining: 1

Exercise 2: <u>Friendly Letter</u>: Write the capitalization and punctuation corrections only.

927 pickwick drive

alex kentucky 40201

aug 21 20__

dear aunt carol

thank you for the digital camera you gave us for christmas its so much fun to take snapshots

of the new baby mom and i have been putting all the pictures into a scrapbook i cant wait

for you to see it

your grateful niece

photo phyllis

Editing Guide:	Capitals: 17	Commas: 4	Periods: 1	Apostrophes: 2	End Marks: 4

Exercise 3: Name the eight parts of speech that you have studied.

1. _____   2. _____   3. _____   4. _____   5. _____   6. _____   7. _____   8. _____

Exercise 4: Identify each pair of words as synonyms or antonyms by putting parentheses ( ) around *syn* or *ant*.

1. knoll, mound	syn ant	5. void, vacant	syn ant	9. mandatory, required	syn ant
2. myth, fact	syn ant	6. perpetual, constant	syn ant	10. spontaneous, forced	syn ant
3. ethical, carnal	syn ant	7. solicitude, indifference	syn ant	11. repulsive, amiable	syn ant
4. truth, veracity	syn ant	8. escalate, expand	syn ant	12. reprehensible, admirable	syn ant

Exercise 5: Underline the correct homonym in each sentence.

1. The pastor knelt at the (altar, alter).
2. We have a beautiful (calendar, calender) in our office.
3. The teacher (cent, sent, scent) her to the office.
4. Mary was (confident, confidant) that she would win the award.
5. Sam loves chocolate (desert, dessert).
6. The books were a (fare, fair) price.
7. The pipes were full of (leaks, leeks).
8. My mother had a (tear, tier) in her eye.

Exercise 6: In your journal, write a paragraph summarizing what you have learned this week.

Chapter 11 Test B

Exercise 1: Classify each sentence.

1. _____ In an argumentative tone, they debated mercilessly about their senior trip.

2. _____ Wait at the crosswalk for the traffic light during the procession.

3. _____ An unbelievable number of inmates recently escaped from the prison farm.

Exercise 2: Sentence: Write the capitalization and punctuation corrections only.

1. i thought of the titanic when larry ricky and i boarded our ship for russia

Editing Guide:	Capitals: 6	Commas: 2	Underline: 1	End Marks: 1

Exercise 3: <u>Friendly Letter</u>: Write the capitalization and punctuation rule numbers for each correction in bold.

20178 **N**orth **B**irch **S**treet

Russell **F**alls, **O**regon 91218

May 23, 20—

Dear **M**artin**,**

I just graduated from college with my degree in medicine. **I** am now **Dr. L**ee. **I** can hardly

believe it! **I**t seems like just yesterday that we walked across the platform at **W**estville **S**tadium.

Do you remember when **Mr. H**arding handed us our high school diploma? **T**hose were the days!

I am looking forward to coming to your graduation soon. **B**est wishes, **Dr. A**dams!

Your best bud**,**

Allen **L**ee

Editing Guide:	Capitals: 28	Commas: 5	Periods: 3	End Marks: 8

Chapter 12 Test

Exercise 1: Classify each sentence.

1. _____ Steve challenges all new opponents quite convincingly.

2. _____ Today, the driver of the blue convertible passed and sideswiped Eleanor's van.

3. _____ Horrors! The hurricane uprooted towering palms and ancient oaks during its savage attack on the coastline!

Exercise 2: Use Sentence 3 to underline the complete subject once and the complete predicate twice and to complete the table below.

List the Noun Used	List the Noun Job	Singular or Plural	Common or Proper	Simple Subject	Simple Predicate
1.	2.	3.	4.	5.	6.
7.	8.	9.	10.		
11.	12.	13.	14.		
15.	16.	17.	18.		
19.	20.	21.	22.		

Exercise 3: Identify each pair of words as synonyms or antonyms by putting parentheses ( ) around **_syn_** or **_ant_**.

1. mimic, imitate	syn	ant	5. wasteful, prodigal	syn	ant	9. ecstatic, blissful	syn	ant
2. stable, precarious	syn	ant	6. savory, bland	syn	ant	10. mandatory, required	syn	ant
3. abolish, destroy	syn	ant	7. odd, quaint	syn	ant	11. marginal, significant	syn	ant
4. alliance, division	syn	ant	8. balloon, zeppelin	syn	ant	12. repulsive, amiable	syn	ant

Exercise 4: Underline the correct homonym in each sentence.

1. Give dad a (piece, peace) of pie.
2. My knee is very (weak, week) after surgery.
3. We parked (by, buy) a black truck.
4. Are we meeting (here, hear) today?
5. Our house has (lead, led) pipes.
6. My sister (blew, blue) her nose loudly.
7. Juneau is the (capital, capitol) of Alaska.
8. Days of the week start with a (capital, capitol) letter.

Exercise 5: <u>For Sentences 1 and 2:</u> Write the capitalization and punctuation corrections only.
<u>For Sentence 3:</u> Write the capitalization and punctuation rule numbers for each correction in bold.

1. lucy did the russian immigrants see sioux falls south dakota on their way to the grand canyon

Editing Guide: Capitals: 8	Commas: 3	End Marks: 1

2. no mr davis and i did not go to a mexican restaurant in santa fe new mexico in june

Editing Guide: Capitals: 10	Commas: 3	Periods: 1	End Marks: 1

3. **O**ur guide**,** **Mr. J. C. N**otingham**,** took us hiking around **L**ake **C**onway near **D**enver**,** **C**olorado**.**

Editing Guide: Capitals: 9	Commas: 3	Periods: 3	End Marks: 1

Exercise 6: In your journal, write a paragraph summarizing what you have learned this week.

Chapter 13 Test

Exercise 1: Classify each sentence.

1. _____ Across the street, the builders quickly erected a retaining wall.

2. _____ Bill and Rhonda rode a city bus to the concert in the park.

Exercise 2: Use Sentence 2 to underline the complete subject once and the complete predicate twice and to complete the table below.

List the Noun Used	List the Noun Job	Singular or Plural	Common or Proper	Simple Subject	Simple Predicate
1.	2.	3.	4.	5.	6.
7.	8.	9.	10.		
11.	12.	13.	14.		
15.	16.	17.	18.		
19.	20.	21.	22.		

Exercise 3: Identify each pair of words as synonyms or antonyms by putting parentheses ( ) around *syn* or *ant*.

1. ecstatic, blissful	syn ant	5. bracelet, bangle	syn ant	9. proverbial, notorious	syn ant
2. innate, acquired	syn ant	6. knoll, mound	syn ant	10. entourage, followers	syn ant
3. audacious, timid	syn ant	7. precarious, stable	syn ant	11. luminous, obscure	syn ant
4. burn, smolder	syn ant	8. zeppelin, balloon	syn ant	12. marginal, significant	syn ant

Exercise 4: Put a slash to separate each run-on sentence below. Then, correct the run-on sentences by rewriting them as indicated by the labels in parentheses at the end of each sentence.

1. Horns were honking sirens were blaring. (**CD**;)

2. The girls washed the windows the boys washed the windows. (**SCS**)

3. The secretary signed the letters she stuffed them in envelopes. (**SCV**)

4. The secretary signed the letters she stuffed them in envelopes. (**CD**, and)

5. Ray rebuilt the fence Warren helped him. (**SCS**)

6. The girls boiled a dozen eggs they colored them for Easter. (**SCV**)

Exercise 5: Identify each kind of sentence by writing the abbreviation in the blank. (**S, F, SCS, SCV, CD**)

_____ 1. The August drought left the lake nearly dry.

_____ 2. She tried to volunteer; yet no one would give her a chance.

_____ 3. The hoe and shovel will go with me to the garden.

_____ 4. Wrapped around the electric pole at the end of our street.

_____ 5. My aunt died; consequently, I have a trip to make.

_____ 6. The usher held her hand and led her to her seat.

_____ 7. Only because we had no other choice.

Exercise 6: On a sheet of paper, write one sentence for each of these labels: (**S**) (**SCS**) (**SCV**) (**CD**).

Exercise 7: In your journal, write a paragraph summarizing what you have learned this week.

Chapter 14 Test

Exercise 1: Classify each sentence.

1. _____ Henry rode a motorcycle to his interviews in Kansas and Nebraska.

2. _____ After twenty years, the congregation surprised him with an

appreciation banquet.

Exercise 2: Use Sentence 2 to underline the complete subject once and the complete predicate twice and to complete the table below.

List the Noun Used	List the Noun Job	Singular or Plural	Common or Proper	Simple Subject	Simple Predicate
1.	2.	3.	4.	5.	6.
7.	8.	9.	10.		
11.	12.	13.	14.		

Exercise 3: Identify each pair of words as synonyms or antonyms by putting parentheses ( ) around *syn* or *ant*.

1. rider, equestrian	syn	ant	5. honesty, integrity	syn	ant	9. equilibrium, balance	syn	ant
2. timid, audacious	syn	ant	6. zeppelin, balloon	syn	ant	10. construction, dilapidation	syn	ant
3. cordial, hostile	syn	ant	7. frivolous, grave	syn	ant	11. solicitude, indifference	syn	ant
4. odious, hateful	syn	ant	8. escalate, expand	syn	ant	12. impenetrable, vulnerable	syn	ant

Exercise 4: Put a slash to separate each run-on sentence below. Then, correct the run-on sentences by rewriting them as indicated by the labels in parentheses at the end of each sentence.

1. The pigs ate all the corn they seemed contented. (**CX**, after 1)

2. The pigs ate all the corn they seemed contented. (**CD**, and)

3. The pigs ate all the corn they seemed contented. (**SCV**)

4. The pigs ate all the corn they seemed contented. (**CD**;)

5. The pigs ate all the corn the chickens ate all the corn. (**SCS**)

Exercise 5: Identify each kind of sentence by writing the abbreviation in the blank (**S, F, SCS, SCV, CD, CX**)

_____ 1. She lost her billfold; moreover, she lost her keys.
_____ 2. When the doorbell rang, she nearly jumped out of her shoes.
_____ 3. Students and teachers alike were ready for vacation.
_____ 4. Whenever I get the oil changed.
_____ 5. My pen is out of ink, and I have no stamps.
_____ 6. Besides being home for Christmas.
_____ 7. Jared drove his truck into the creek and got stuck.

Exercise 6: On notebook paper, write three complex sentences. Underline each <u>subordinate</u> sentence.

Exercise 7: On notebook paper, write one sentence for each of these labels: (**S**) (**SCS**) (**SCV**) (**CD**) (**CX**).

Exercise 8: In your journal, write a paragraph summarizing what you have learned this week.

Chapter 15 Test

Exercise 1: Classify each sentence.

1. _____ Two skillful, dedicated pastors built a small church on the land behind our farm.

2. _____ The energetic children have collected papers and magazines at church.

Exercise 2: Use Sentence 1 to underline the complete subject once and the complete predicate twice and to complete the table below.

List the Noun Used	List the Noun Job	Singular or Plural	Common or Proper	Simple Subject	Simple Predicate
1.	2.	3.	4.	5.	6.
7.	8.	9.	10.		
11.	12.	13.	14.		
15.	16.	17.	18.		

Exercise 3: Identify each pair of words as synonyms or antonyms by putting parentheses ( ) around **syn** or **ant**.

1. thrifty, frugal	syn ant	5. rider, equestrian	syn ant	9. fatigue, exhaustion	syn ant
2. argue, debate	syn ant	6. gullible, dubious	syn ant	10. cordial, hostile	syn ant
3. gaudy, tasteful	syn ant	7. fact, hypothesis	syn ant	11. grandiose, impressive	syn ant
4. prodigy, genius	syn ant	8. bracelet, bangle	syn ant	12. innate, acquired	syn ant

Exercise 4: Part A: Underline each noun to be made possessive and write singular or plural (**S-P**), the rule number, and the possessive form. Part B: Write each noun as singular possessive and then as plural possessive.

1. For a singular noun - add (**'s**)		2. For a plural noun that ends in **s** - add (**'**)		3. For a plural noun that does not end in **s** - add (**'s**)		
Rule 1: boy's		**Rule 2: boys'**		**Rule 3: men's**		
Part A	**S-P**	**Rule**	**Possessive Form**	**Part B**	**Singular Poss**	**Plural Poss**
1. flags waving				12. ax		
2. Dennis courtesy				13. roof		
3. fence height				14. wolf		
4. diner menu				15. cousin		
5. letter intent				16. turkey		
6. fielders errors				17. child		
7. judge verdict				18. mirror		
8. parents worries				19. gentleman		
9. flight delay				20. pirate		
10. crows footprints				21. igloo		
11. barbers prices				22. woman		

Exercise 5: On a sheet of paper, write one sentence for each of these labels: (**S**) (**SCS**) (**SCV**) (**CD**) (**CX**).

Exercise 6: In your journal, write a paragraph summarizing what you have learned this week.

Chapter 16 Test

Exercise 1: Classify each sentence.

1. _____ Give your cousin those sparkly earrings for her birthday.

2. _____ The waiter at the new restaurant served us an excellent dessert.

3. _____ Have you given Gene and Laura the note from your mom?

Exercise 2: Use Sentence 3 to underline the complete subject once and the complete predicate twice and to complete the table below.

List the Noun Used	List the Noun Job	Singular or Plural	Common or Proper	Simple Subject	Simple Predicate
1.	2.	3.	4.	5.	6.
7.	8.	9.	10.		
11.	12.	13.	14.		
15.	16.	17.	18.		

Exercise 3: Identify each pair of words as synonyms or antonyms by putting parentheses ( ) around *syn* or *ant*.

1. odd, quaint	syn ant	5. flippant, polite	syn ant	9. scrutinize, examine	syn ant
2. ethical, carnal	syn ant	6. exquisite, gauche	syn ant	10. impenetrable, vulnerable	syn ant
3. mimic, imitate	syn ant	7. gullible, dubious	syn ant	11. conceal, camouflage	syn ant
4. gaudy, tasteful	syn ant	8. prodigal, wasteful	syn ant	12. luminous, obscure	syn ant

Exercise 4: Underline the correct homonym in each sentence.

1. We drove (threw, through) the tunnel at night.

2. The kitten cut (its, it's) paw on the barbed wire.

3. Put (your, you're) pajamas in my suitcase.

4. He has been our (principal, principle) for ten years now.

5. It is so easy (to, too, two) throw caution to the wind.

6. He seemed to be on the right (coarse, course) for success.

Exercise 5: Identify these pronouns by writing **S** (subjective), **O** (objective), or **P** (possessive) in each blank.

____ 1. their ____ 2. our ____ 3. we ____ 4. them ____ 5. it ____ 6. us ____ 7. your ___ 8. she

Exercise 6: For Sentences 1-4, replace each underlined pronoun by writing the correct form in the first blank and **S** or **O** for subjective or objective case in the second blank.

1. No one asked Jim or I. _____ _____

2. It is too cold for we. _____ _____

3. The principal summoned they to the office. _____ _____

4. Mark and her are dating now. _____ _____

Exercise 7: Identify each kind of sentence by writing the abbreviation in the blank. (**S**, **F**, **SCS**, **SCV**, **CD**, **CX**)

_____ 1. As long as there are no detours.

_____ 2. The jalopy coughed and sputtered to a stop.

_____ 3. I forgot her number; moreover, I don't have time to call.

_____ 4. Because the ice storm came, travel was imperiled.

_____ 5. The post office and jail were destroyed in the fire.

Exercise 8: There are three ways to connect compound sentences. Write a sentence demonstrating each one.

Exercise 9: In your journal, write a paragraph summarizing what you have learned this week.

Chapter 17 Test

Exercise 1: Classify each sentence.

1. _____ Give Jim and Ed the directions to your summer camp.

2. _____ The guard calmly gave the inmates detailed instructions about their release.

Exercise 2: Use Sentence 1 to underline the complete subject once and the complete predicate twice and to complete the table below.

List the Noun Used	List the Noun Job	Singular or Plural	Common or Proper	Simple Subject	Simple Predicate
1.	2.	3.	4.	5.	6.
7.	8.	9.	10.		
11.	12.	13.	14.		
15.	16.	17.	18.		

Exercise 3: Identify each pair of words as synonyms or antonyms by putting parentheses ( ) around *syn* or *ant*.

1. ecstatic, blissful	syn ant	5. precarious, stable	syn ant	9. contemplate, ponder	syn ant
2. cordial, hostile	syn ant	6. withhold, bequeath	syn ant	10. entourage, followers	syn ant
3. delusion, reality	syn ant	7. diligent, negligent	syn ant	11. enunciate, pronounce	syn ant
4. bangle, bracelet	syn ant	8. mandatory, required	syn ant	12. veritable, fictitious	syn ant

Exercise 4: For Sentences 1-4, replace each underlined pronoun by writing the correct form in the first blank and **S** or **O** for subjective or objective case in the second blank.

1. Invite Velma and I sometime. _____ _____
2. Mike and me ate pizza last night. _____ _____
3. Winter gave my sister and I colds. _____ _____
4. The finalists were Boyd and me. _____ _____

Exercise 5: Use the Quotation Rules to help punctuate the quotations below. Underline the explanatory words.

1. why did i think you were a cowboy inquired tom with a smile

2. when i was younger i was ronnie replied

3. so tom said what do you do now if i might ask

4. looking tom straight in the eye ronnie retorted i haul cotton in kennett missouri

Exercise 6: On notebook paper, write one sentence for each of these labels: **(S) (SCS) (SCV) (CD) (CX)**.

Exercise 7: On notebook paper, write three sentences, demonstrating each of the three quotations: Beginning quote, end quote, and split quote.

Exercise 8: In your journal, write a paragraph summarizing what you have learned this week.

Chapter 18A Test

Exercise 1: Classify each sentence.

1. _____ Kim packed Gary and me broccoli and cauliflower for our snack at work.

2. _____ Would you fax me your purchase order on Monday?

Exercise 2: Use Sentence 2 to underline the complete subject once and the complete predicate twice and to complete the table below.

List the Noun Used	List the Noun Job	Singular or Plural	Common or Proper	Simple Subject	Simple Predicate
1.	2.	3.	4.	5.	6.
7.	8.	9.	10.		

Exercise 3: Identify each pair of words as synonyms or antonyms by putting parentheses ( ) around **syn** or **ant**.

1. veracity, truth	syn ant	5. forfeit, relinquish	syn ant	9. grandiose, impressive	syn ant
2. vanquish, escape	syn ant	6. deception, candor	syn ant	10. solicitude, indifference	syn ant
3. coherent, ramble	syn ant	7. repulsive, amiable	syn ant	11. transparent, translucent	syn ant
4. solitary, alone	syn ant	8. fatigue, exhaustion	syn ant	12. marginal, significant	syn ant

Exercise 4: Underline each verb or verb phrase. Identify the verb tense by writing a number **1** for present tense, a number **2** for past tense, and a number **3** for future tense. Write the past tense form and **R** or **I** for Regular or Irregular.

Verb Tense		Main Verb Past Tense Form	R or I
2	1. He purchased the house at auction.	Purchased	R
	2. Will you walk home?		
	3. I have eaten already.		
	4. He stands alone on the issue.		
	5. You will be receiving a subpoena.		
	6. She is painting her toenails.		
	7. My sister swallowed the gum.		
	8. We had driven all night.		
	9. He will fly to the islands.		
	10. He had combined wheat before.		
	11. Roy has left the team again.		
	12. She has written me before.		

Exercise 5: Identify each kind of sentence by writing the abbreviation in the blank. (**S**, **F**, **SCS**, **SCV**, **CD**, **CX**)

_____ 1. The boys and girls stood in line almost an hour.

_____ 2. We can't get out when the road is flooded.

_____ 3. The wasp attacked and stung me on the arm.

_____ 4. The canoe in the middle of the river.

_____ 5. The tickets are too expensive; besides, I have another commitment.

Chapter 18B Test

Exercise 6: Change the underlined present tense verbs in Paragraph 1 to past tense verbs in Paragraph 2.

Paragraph 1: Present Tense

Grandma **makes** applesauce every October. She **gathers** apples from the trees in her orchard.   She **places** them in her summer kitchen to ripen. Once they **are** ripe, she **removes** the cores and **quarters** them. She barely **covers** the fruit with water and **cooks** it on low heat until it **is** mushy. Then, she **strains** it through a colander and **adds** the necessary spices to give it a tangy flavor.

Paragraph 2: Past Tense

Grandma _____ applesauce every October. She _____ apples from the trees in her orchard. She _____ them in her summer kitchen to ripen. Once they _____ ripe, she _____ the cores and _____ them. She barely _____ the fruit with water and _____ it on low heat until it _____ mushy. Then, she _____ it through a colander and _____ the necessary spices to give it a tangy flavor.

Exercise 7: Change the underlined mixed tense verbs in Paragraph 1 to present tense verbs in Paragraph 2.

Paragraph 1: Mixed Tenses

Our mother **played** with dolls. She **designs** their clothes, houses, and cars. She **laughed** at night as she **tells** us about their adventures. She **brought** home examples of new products. We **gather** excitedly around the table as she **demonstrated** the newest fashions and trends. Our mother **hugged** us to her and **tells** us the same thing every night. We **were** her most precious dolls!

Paragraph 2: Present Tense

Our mother _____with dolls. She_____ their clothes, houses, and cars. She_____ at night as she _____ us about their adventures. She_____home examples of new products. We_____ excitedly around the table as she_____the newest fashions and trends. Our mother_____ us to her and _____us the same thing every night. We _____ her most precious dolls!

Exercise 8: On notebook paper, write one sentence for each of these labels: **(S)** **(SCS)** **(SCV)** **(CD)** **(CX)**.

Exercise 9: On notebook paper, write three sentences, demonstrating each of the three quotations: Beginning quote, end quote, and split quote.

Exercise 10: On notebook paper, write the seven present tense helping verbs, the five past tense helping verbs, and the two future tense helping verbs.

Exercise 11: In your journal, write a paragraph summarizing what you have learned this week.

Chapter 19 Test

Exercise 1: Classify each sentence.

1. _____ The iguana is a large tropical lizard of the Iguanidae family.

2. _____ Sue was a missionary in Africa.

3. _____ The sunset is a very lovely sight.

Exercise 2: Identify each pair of words as synonyms or antonyms by putting parentheses ( ) around *syn* or *ant*.

1. burn, smolder	syn	ant	5. adversity, misfortune	syn	ant	9. contemplate, ponder	syn	ant
2. flippant, polite	syn	ant	6. delusion, reality	syn	ant	10. colleague, competitor	syn	ant
3. exquisite, gauche	syn	ant	7. conceited, humble	syn	ant	11. equilibrium, balance	syn	ant
4. creditor, lender	syn	ant	8. scrutinize, examine	syn	ant	12. contemptible, admirable	syn	ant

Exercise 3: Change the underlined mixed tense verbs in Paragraph 1 to past tense verbs in Paragraph 2.

Paragraph 1: Mixed Tenses

Bolivar **is** my constant companion. He **followed** me everywhere I **go** and **protects** me from potential harm. He **loved** the attention I **give** him and **likes** to be petted. We **take** long walks in the woods on warm days and often **sat** on the bank of the pond where we **listen** to a chorus of frogs.

Paragraph 2: Past Tense

Bolivar _____ my constant companion. He _____ me everywhere I _____ and _____ me from potential harm. He _____ the attention I _____ him and _____ to be petted. We _____ long walks in the woods on warm days and often _____ on the bank of the pond where we _____ to a chorus of frogs.

Exercise 4: Copy the following words on notebook paper. Write the correct contraction beside each word.
Words: you have, there is, is not, they will, will not, it is, he will, let us, we would, I will, you will, was not, do not, they have, I am, does not, have not.

Exercise 5: Copy the following contractions on notebook paper. Write the correct words beside each contraction.
Contractions: they're, he's, you're, hasn't, you'd, we've, doesn't, hadn't, can't, I'd, don't.

Exercise 6: Write the seven present tense helping verbs, the five past tense helping verbs, and the two future tense helping verbs.

Exercise 7: In your journal, write a paragraph summarizing what you have learned this week.

Chapter 20 Test

Exercise 1: Classify each sentence.

1. _____ My cousin's last two dogs were Dalmatians.

2. _____ During the storm, the tourists became guests of the hotel for three days.

Exercise 2: Identify each pair of words as synonyms or antonyms by putting parentheses ( ) around **syn** or **ant**.

1. delusion, reality	syn	ant	4. vanquish, escape	syn	ant	7. expense, disbursement	syn	ant
2. solitary, alone	syn	ant	5. component, whole	syn	ant	8. mandatory, required	syn	ant
3. candid, sly	syn	ant	6. creditor, lender	syn	ant	9. contemptible, admirable	syn	ant

Exercise 3: Underline the negative words in each sentence. Rewrite each sentence and correct the double negative mistake as indicated by the rule number in parentheses at the end of the sentence.

Rule 1	**Rule 2**	**Rule 3**
Change the second negative to a positive.	Take out the negative part of a contraction.	Remove the first negative word (verb change).

1. Amy doesn't never stay home. (Rule 3)

_____

2. Matt doesn't have no excuse. (Rule 1)

_____

3. I won't say nothing to her. (Rule 1)

_____

4. We didn't do nothing wrong. (Rule 3)

_____

5. He couldn't see nothing in the dark. (Rule 1)

_____

6. My dad wouldn't never dispute my mom's word. (Rule 2)

_____

7. Tommy can't find no scissors. (Rule 2)

_____

8. Earl doesn't never answer the phone. (Rule 3)

_____

Exercise 4: Write the rule numbers and the different forms for the adjectives below. For irregular forms, write **Irr**.

Comparative: Rule 1: Use **-er** with 1 or 2 syllable words and **more** with -ful words, awkward words, or words with 3 or more syllables.
Superlative: Rule 2: Use **-est** with 1 or 2 syllable words and **most** with -ful words, awkward words, or words with 3 or more syllables.

Simple Adjective Form	Rule Box	Comparative Adjective Form	Rule Box	Superlative Adjective Form
1. cold				
2. bad				
3. brave				
4. inventive				
5. many				
6. warm				
7. apparent				

Exercise 5: In each blank, write the correct form of the adjective in parentheses to complete the sentences.

1. Annette was the _____ student in the class. (attentive)

2. Mrs. Montgomery was _____ substitute. (wonderful)

3. Lisa is _____ than her sister. (young)

4. Metal parts are _____ than plastic. (durable)

Exercise 6: In your journal, write a paragraph summarizing what you have learned this week.

Chapter 21 Test

Exercise 1: Classify each sentence.

1. _____ My uncle's impressive stamp collection is a noteworthy item.

2. _____ Meat and vegetables are essential ingredients of all our meals.

Exercise 2: Identify each pair of words as synonyms or antonyms by putting parentheses ( ) around **syn** or **ant**.

1. diligent, negligent	syn	ant	4. brusque, diplomatic	syn	ant	7. enunciation, pronounce	syn	ant
2. deception, candor	syn	ant	5. superficial, genuine	syn	ant	8. camouflage, conceal	syn	ant
3. aggressive, hostile	syn	ant	6. amateur, beginner	syn	ant	9. melodramatic, subdued	syn	ant

Exercise 3: Choose an answer from the choices in parentheses. Fill in the other columns according to the titles.
(**S** or **P** stands for singular or plural.)

Pronoun-antecedent agreement

	Pronoun Choice	S or P	Antecedent	S or P
1. The books on the shelves are missing (its, their) dust jackets.				
2. His petition for repeal lost (its, their) appeal.				
3. The foreign missionaries lost (his, their) plane tickets.				
4. Ultimately, the fever ran (its, their) course.				

Exercise 4: Underline the negative words in each sentence. Rewrite each sentence and correct the double negative mistake as indicated by the rule number in parentheses at the end of the sentence.

Rule 1	**Rule 2**	**Rule 3**
Change the second negative to a positive.	Take out the negative part of a contraction.	Remove the first negative word (verb change).

1. She didn't want no sympathy. (Rule 3)

_____

2. They don't never take a lunch break. (Rule 3)

_____

3. He wasn't never unruly. (Rule 2)

_____

4. Mom didn't get no bread at the store. (Rule 1)

_____

Exercise 5: On notebook paper, write three sentences, demonstrating each of the three degrees of adjectives. Identify the form you used by writing **simple, comparative,** or **superlative** at the end of each sentence.

Exercise 6: On notebook paper, write three sentences in which you demonstrate each of the double negative rules. Underline the negative word in each sentence.

Exercise 7: Write the seven present tense helping verbs, the five past tense helping verbs, and the two future tense helping verbs.

Exercise 8: On notebook paper, write one sentence for each of these labels: **(S) (SCS) (SCV) (CD) (CX)**.

Exercise 9: In your journal, write a paragraph summarizing what you have learned this week.

Chapter 22 Test

Exercise 1: Classify each sentence.

1. _____ Diet and exercise are the central focus of wellness.

2. _____ The president of our organization went to South America and talked about peace.

3. _____ The sirens gave us a warning about the approaching tornado!

Exercise 2: Use Sentence 3 to underline the complete subject once and the complete predicate twice and complete the table below.

List the Noun Used	List the Noun Job	Singular or Plural	Common or Proper	Simple Subject	Simple Predicate
1.	2.	3.	4.	5.	6.
7.	8.	9.	10.		
11.	12.	13.	14.		

Exercise 3: Identify each pair of words as synonyms or antonyms by putting parentheses ( ) around **syn** or **ant**.

1. summit, base	syn	ant	4. component, whole	syn	ant	7. forfeit, relinquish	syn	ant
2. repeal, pass	syn	ant	5. chaperon, escort	syn	ant	8. brusque, diplomatic	syn	ant
3. attire, apparel	syn	ant	6. adversity, misfortune	syn	ant	9. expense, disbursement	syn	ant

Exercise 4: Write the rule numbers from Reference 66 on page 44 and the correct plural forms of the nouns below.

		Rule	Plural Form			Rule	Plural Form
1.	witch			10.	donkey		
2.	rodeo			11.	ox		
3.	wolf			12.	pony		
4.	goose			13.	fish		
5.	livery			14.	ally		
6.	potato			15.	alley		
7.	deer			16.	child		
8.	wife			17.	moose		
9.	roof			18.	fox		

Exercise 5: Underline each subject and fill in each column according to the title.

1. Wild onions are poisonous.

2. Honesty is a virtue.

3. Virgil won the race.

4. Milk is rich in Vitamin D.

5. Grandma is the family matriarch.

List each Verb	Write PrN, PA, or None	Write L or A

Exercise 6: On notebook paper, make a list of twelve contractions, then write the words from which the contractions come.

Exercise 7: In your journal, write a paragraph summarizing what you have learned this week.

Chapter 23 Test

Exercise 1: Classify each sentence.

1. _____ The giant white bell rang continuously from the large steeple.

2. _____ Rachel and I have preached many sermons during our missionary trip.

Exercise 2: Identify each pair of words as synonyms or antonyms by putting parentheses ( ) around **syn** or **ant**.

1. provoke, pacify	syn	ant	4. superficial, genuine	syn	ant	7. mandatory, required	syn	ant
2. reconcile, sever	syn	ant	5. reimburse, refund	syn	ant	8. amateur, beginner	syn	ant
3. reputable, honest	syn	ant	6. conceited, humble	syn	ant	9. precarious, stable	syn	ant

Exercise 3: Choose an answer from the choices in parentheses. Then, fill in the rest of the columns according to the titles. (**S** or **P** stands for singular or plural.)

Pronoun-antecedent agreement

1. The turtles in the woods are burying (its, their) eggs.
2. The stewardess lost (her, their) oxygen mask.
3. A letter in the mailbox lost (its, their) stamp.
4. My cousins misplaced (its, their) shoes.
5. The ice cream lost (its, their) flavor.
6. The immigrants gained (its, their) citizenship last week.
7. Everything in the files is in (its, their) place.
8. The mayor handed the gavel to (his, their) successor.

Pronoun Choice	S or P	Antecedent	S or P

Exercise 4: Underline each subject and fill in each column according to the title.

1. Viruses are contagious.
2. Kyle is this year's winner.
3. Accidents are unavoidable.
4. Flags fly from the capitol dome.
5. Her umbrella was a lifesaver.

List each Verb	Write PrN, PA, or None	Write L or A

Exercise 5: On notebook paper, write the seven present tense helping verbs, the five past tense helping verbs, and the two future tense helping verbs.

Exercise 6: On notebook paper, write three sentences, demonstrating each of the three degrees of adjectives. Identify the form you used by writing **simple, comparative,** or **superlative** at the end of each sentence.

Exercise 7: On notebook paper, identify the parts of a friendly letter and envelope by writing the titles and an example for each title. Use References 67 and 68 to help you.

Exercise 8: In your journal, write a paragraph summarizing what you have learned this week.

Chapter 24 Test

Exercise 1: Classify each sentence.

1. _____ The pies from the pastry shop are a tasty and delightful dessert.

2. _____ A strong, young guide took us down the wild rapids.

Exercise 2: Identify each pair of words as synonyms or antonyms by putting parentheses ( ) around **syn** or **ant**.

1. noble, paltry	syn	ant	4. provoke, pacify	syn	ant	7. reputable, honest	syn	ant
2. reconcile, sever	syn	ant	5. abscond, escape	syn	ant	8. reimburse, refund	syn	ant
3. vile, repulsive	syn	ant	6. notorious, reputed	syn	ant	9. candid, sly	syn	ant

Exercise 3: Underline each subject and fill in each column according to the title.

	List each Verb	Write PrN, PA, or None	Write L or A
1. Popsicles are refreshing.			
2. This address is incorrect.			
3. Sandi ate her orange outdoors.			
4. Novels are lengthy stories.			

Exercise 4: Choose an answer from the choices in parentheses. Then, fill in the rest of the columns according to the titles. (**S** or **P** stands for singular or plural.)

Pronoun-antecedent agreement

	Pronoun Choice	S or P	Antecedent	S or P
1. The lions in the cage are venting (its, their) anger.				
2. The president of the group lost (her, their) notes.				
3. Wyoming lost (its, their) claim to copper.				
4. Clifton gave (his, their) approval to the purchase.				

Exercise 5: On notebook paper, identify the parts of a business letter and envelope by writing the titles and an example for each title. Use References 70 and 71 to help you.

Exercise 6: On notebook paper, write three sentences, demonstrating each of the three degrees of adjectives. Identify the form you used by writing **simple, comparative,** or **superlative** at the end of each sentence.

Exercise 7: On notebook paper, write one sentence for each of these labels: **(S) (SCS) (SCV) (CD) (CX)**.

Exercise 8: On notebook paper, write three sentences in which you demonstrate each of the double negative rules. Underline the negative word in each sentence. (Use your book for the double negative rules.)

Exercise 9: In your journal, write a paragraph summarizing what you have learned this week.

Chapter 25 Test

Exercise 1: Classify each sentence.

1. _____ Bible scholars are constantly documenting new research.

2. _____ Cindy is not going to the golf tournament today.

Exercise 2: Write a thank-you note. First, think of a person who has done something nice for you or has given you a gift (even the gift of time). Next, write that person a thank-you note using the information in the Reference section as a guide.

Exercise 3: Make an invitation card. First, think of a special event or occasion and who will be invited. Next, make an invitation to send out, using the information in the Reference section as a guide. Illustrate your card appropriately.

Exercise 4: On notebook paper, write the seven present tense helping verbs, the five past tense helping verbs, and the two future tense helping verbs.

Exercise 5: On notebook paper, write three sentences, demonstrating each of the three degrees of adjectives. Identify the form you used by writing **simple, comparative,** or **superlative** at the end of each sentence.

Exercise 6: On notebook paper, write three sentences in which you demonstrate each of the double negative rules. Underline the negative word in each sentence. (Use your book for the double negative rules.)

Exercise 7: In your journal, write a paragraph summarizing what you have learned this week.

Chapter 26 Test

Exercise 1: Classify each sentence.

1. _____ Will Mrs. Green give you a music lesson?

2. _____ The band conductor lost money on his trip.

Exercise 2: Match each part of a book listed below with the type of information it may give you. Write the appropriate letter in the blank. You may use a letter only once.

A. Title page	B. Copyright page	C. Index	D. Bibliography	E. Appendix	F. Glossary

1. _____ A list of books used by the author as references

2. _____ Meanings of important words in the book

3. _____ Publisher's name and city where the book was published

4. _____ ISBN number

5. _____ Used to locate topics quickly

6. _____ Extra maps in a book

Exercise 3: Match each part of a book listed below with the type of information it may give you. Write the appropriate letter in the blank. You may use a letter only once.

A. Title page	B. Table of contents	C. Copyright page	D. Index	E. Bibliography
F. Preface	G. Body			

1. _____ Exact page numbers for a particular topic

2. _____ Author's name, title of book, and illustrator's name

3. _____ Books listed for finding more information

4. _____ Text of the book

5. _____ Reason the book was written

6. _____ Titles of units and chapters

7. _____ Copyright date

Exercise 4: Write the five parts found at the front of a book.

1. _____ 2. _____ 3. _____ 4. _____ 5. _____

Exercise 5: Write the four parts found at the back of a book.

1. _____ 2. _____ 3. _____ 4. _____

Exercise 6: Underline each subject and fill in each column according to the title.

	List each Verb	Write PrN, PA, or None	Write L or A
1. The iris is a beautiful flower.			
2. The venison was delicious.			
3. Leah's mom called for help.			
4. Maine is a fishing state.			
5. Harp music is very soothing.			

Exercise 7: In your journal, write a paragraph summarizing what you have learned this week.

Chapter 27A Test

Exercise 1: Classify each sentence.

1. _____ Fred opened the door to the cellar with a crowbar.

2. _____ Dorothy's costume was the highlight of the evening.

Exercise 2: Underline each subject and fill in each column according to the title.

	List each Verb	Write PrN, PA, or None	Write L or A
1. Jerky is very chewy.			
2. The siren startled the pedestrians.			
3. Waycross is a small town.			
4. Motel rooms are expensive.			

Exercise 3: Use the Table of Contents example in Reference 77 to answer the following questions.

1. Look over the chapter titles. What is this book about?
2. How many chapters are in this book?
3. What is the last page of Chapter 1?
4. You are considering becoming a trucker, just like your dad. What two chapters might give you the best insight into what you might need to know to make a career choice?
5. Your dad will be home next week. You want to know what life will be like for him during his break. What chapter would you look in for insights?
6. Your dad wants to be sure he is in a safe place when he parks his truck at night. Which chapter would you look in for sound advice?
   On which page does that chapter begin?
7. Which chapter would you look at to see how companies schedule long-distance trips for their drivers?
8. Your dad wants to talk to his boss about getting next week off for your birthday. This would involve delaying his trip to Ohio. Which chapter would have information about how he would do this?
9. A roadside rest near Phoenix is the most logical place for your dad to stop on his trip to California. He needs to know whether or not it is advisable to spend the night there. On what page would you begin looking?
10. When your dad gets a week off next month, you'd like to do a few things with him. Which chapter might offer you some suggestions?
11. Bonus: How many pages are in Chapter 3?

Exercise 4: Answer the following questions about an index on another sheet of paper.
1. What are three main reasons to use an index?
2. Where is an index located?
3. How does an index list information?
4. When an index lists key ideas in a book, what are the key ideas called?
5. When an index lists specific information under the topic, what is it called?
6. What do the numbers following topics and subtopics tell?

Chapter 27B Test

Exercise 5: Write the correct answers for numbers 1-6. Underline the correct answer for numbers 7-8.

1. The type of reference one would check for articles on the recent presidential election is what? _____

2. If you don't have the title of a book or an author's name to check, what type of catalog card would you check? _____

3. To plan a safari, one would do well to research the terrain of the country where you're going. What type of reference would provide maps of various countries and continents? _____

4. To find the spellings of homonyms, one would go to what type of reference? _____

5. The type of books arranged numerically on the shelves is what? _____

6. Published annually, this reference provides updates on facts and figures about such things as moon phases, tides, populations, and so on. _____

7. Biographies are arranged on the shelves by (**the name of the author, the person written about**).

8. Fiction books are arranged on the shelves in (**numerical order, alphabetical order**).

Exercise 6: Put the fiction books below in the correct order to go on the shelves. Write numbers 1-7 in the blanks to show the correct order. *(Alphabetize fiction books by authors' last names.)*

1. *The Scarlet Letter* by Nathaniel Hawthorne _____
2. *A Farewell to Arms* by Ernest Hemingway _____
3. *Now in November* by Josephine Johnson _____
4. *The Pathfinder* by James Fenimore Cooper _____
5. *Moby Dick* by Herman Melville _____
6. *The Grapes of Wrath* by John Steinbeck _____
7. *Ulysses* by James Joyce _____

Exercise 7: Write **True** or **False** for each statement.

1. Biographies are arranged on the shelf by the author's last name. _____

2. The call number for books is located in the upper right-hand corner of a catalog card. _____

3. Nonfiction books are arranged on the shelves numerically. _____

4. An almanac is a reference containing maps. _____

5. The title of a book is located on the top line of subject cards and title cards in the card catalog. _____

6. The Reader's Guide to Periodical Literature is an index to magazine articles. _____

7. Books of fiction are arranged alphabetically by the author's last name. _____

8. Encyclopedias are references that provide brief information about people and places and events of worldwide interest. _____

Exercise 8: Draw and label the three catalog cards for this book on a sheet of notebook paper: 843.7 *Poetry's Well-Traveled Roads* by Dan Lindsay, Phoenix Press, Sacramento, 2001, 358 p. *(Use the catalog card examples in Reference 75.)*

Exercise 9: In your journal, write a paragraph summarizing what you have learned this week.

Chapter 28 Test

Exercise 1: Classify each sentence.

1. _____ Most fans were enthusiastically cheering for Travis and me.

2. _____ Four French tourists gave stern lectures to the inconsiderate teens.

3. _____ Will you serve us fried okra for lunch tomorrow?

Exercise 2: Copy the notes below into a three-point outline. Change wording to put notes into correct parallel form.

Notes	Outline
types of poems lyrical poems highly musical sensory narratives built on action dialogue, usually dramatic poems to be read aloud performed on stage	

Exercise 3: On notebook paper, write all the jingles that you can recall from memory. There is a total of 19 jingles.

Exercise 4: In your journal, write a paragraph summarizing what you have learned this week.